We Don't Trust Your Theology

We Don't Trust Your Theology

Reconstructing Your Faith from Rubble

GEORGE M. BENSON

RESOURCE *Publications* • Eugene, Oregon

WE DON'T TRUST YOUR THEOLOGY
Reconstructing Your Faith from Rubble

Resource Publications
An Imprint of Wipf and Stock Publishers
199 W. 8th Ave., Suite 3
Eugene, OR 97401

www.wipfandstock.com

PAPERBACK ISBN: 978-1-6667-0165-4
HARDCOVER ISBN: 978-1-6667-0166-1
EBOOK ISBN: 978-1-6667-0167-8

DECEMBER 17, 2021 8:04 AM

To my wife Jette. There is so much I can say. I love you and without you this would have never happened.
Maybe I'll be less of a pain now that this project is over.
Thank you for being my person.

To Lindsey, the original editor. Thank you for your tireless work in the in this project, and the encouragement.

To Adam, Rob, Devon, and many other friends and family members. Thank you for the texts, emails, phone calls, and confidence.

Also, to Cody, Blinken, and Lil' Sebastian.
While I love you all, your litter boxes are foul.

Jesus Christ, son of God have mercy on me, someone
who has no idea what they are doing and just trying to get through.

Contents

Introduction || *ix*

1   I Still Consider Myself an Evangelical, but Reluctantly || 1

2   "But don't take my word for it, make sure you look it up yourself!" — Your Pastor || 6

3   Sifting Through the Ashes || 12

4   Laying Groundwork on the Bible Part 1 || 16

5   Laying Groundwork on the Bible Part 2 || 23

6   The God of Creation, Destruction, and Recreation || 27

7   The God of Abraham and You! || 36

8   Bible Groundwork Wrap Up || 49

9   The Names of God and What They Say About Them || 52

10 Jesus: Human Trolly Problem, Wrong Place at the Wrong Time, or Someone Completely Different? || 59

11 Reconstructing God and Jesus || 67

12 A New Church for a New Generation || 73

13   Recognizing our Privilege: Prejudice, Racism, Sexism, and Ableism in
      the American Evangelical Church || 80

14   The Gospel . . . also Evangelism || 91

15   The Fire Down Below and the Kin-dom at Hand || 97

16   Growth, Change, and Discipleship || 104

17   This Is Where I Leave You || 108

Appendix A || 113

Bibliography || 115

Introduction

WHO WOULD WRITE A BOOK with a title as outlandish as, *We Don't Trust Your Theology?* To paint a picture, I am a comfortable—in—skin (CIS), heterosexual, able—bodied white male who has benefited time and again from my privilege. The title is almost a direct quote from a former employer, while the conversation at the time was difficult, I remember thinking, "that's a great title, I need to put that away and use it sometime." This book is about leaving white American evangelicalism to a different type of abundance in a God most of my churches have ignored. That is where my primary experience comes from, and if you are picking up this book, I imagine you probably have a similar background. To clarify, when I say white evangelical, I mean a church whose leadership is filled predominately with male caucasians who perpetuate that viewpoint and embrace the patriarchy whole heartily. I should also state that any knowledge I have about Judaism that is shared in this book (unless stated otherwise) is about ancient Judaism. It is not a comment on how Judaism has evolved over the ages and where it currently rests. Also, to my knowledge, everything I am going to lay out in this book is not new under the sun. Parts may have a different spin that were previously presented but to be fair, that is what we do when we ingest new information. We let it live in us before we talk about it with others and refine it. This is just my regurgitation of study, conversations, and consuming books and podcasts.

Back in 2012, I realized the church I was working in, let's call it Fields Community Church, felt more oppressive than liberating. This feeling may not have been shared by everyone, but for me that was the case, and I tried to make it work. I had been burning the candle at both ends, and even though I had a call to be there, it did not feel like it was recognized by a lot of the leadership until it was too late. When I left there I spent the following three years in a place of resentment and anger. Rejecting everything I had learned and feeling like I wasted my time and finances, I slipped into a deep and dark depression. I had thought the church was the hope of the world, and the place that I had been most vulnerable with, had chewed me up and spit me out seemingly without thinking twice. It was a hard season complete with loss of identity, counseling, and terrible coping mechanisms for self—medication. It wasn't until mid—February of 2016 that I had an experience. It was time to get out of the funk and get back in the ministry game.

Luckily, I had a few close friends I could talk to about this, and a wife that knows how to push me and ask the right questions to get going. We were in a small group around this time, at the church we were members in, and it really helped me get back into a safe space and trust those who are in the "church" again. So, faced with finally looking at the flaming garbage fire that was my theology or worldview that I walked away from I had to do something about it. I felt isolated, alone, and honestly not wanting to do anything with it but try and ignore it and move on. Fortunately, this rebuilding of my faith started around the same time I had rekindled a friendship with my mentor, Don. Talking with him helped me really put my thoughts in order and during those times we would talk, he would openly challenge my reassembled ideas. While at times it was extremely frustrating, it proved to be a very beneficial experience. I will state it many times throughout this book but, this work would not exist without two people, and he is one of them.

However, and most importantly, this book would not have happened if it was not for my wife. More often than not, she believes in me more than I do myself, and while there have been times I was left to my own devices, she has never given up on me.

She pulled me out of the darkness, called me on my crap when I was drifting away, and is always the true north of my compass. I wrote this during my longest stretch of unemployment, and she knew when to encourage me to take a break with working on our house or applying for jobs with no luck. Forced me out of the door for coffee dates where I could write, and encouraged me to finally say what had been building up for many, many years.

Over the course of the past few years, I have found myself in situations and conversations where I would be sitting across the bar or coffee shop from someone who would either be in the beginning, midst of, or completing deconstruction. To be clear, for the purposes of this book, when I say deconstruction, what I mean is the act of going through one's faith and either lightly removing or completely bulldozing theology that no longer holds water. Things that people have held on to from the beginning of their faith journey and no longer find useful or fits because they opened a book, or dared to ask, "why is it this way?" While most of the time I did not want to talk to them because I had other things I was trying to accomplish, inevitably we would chat. We'd chat about how large the idea of faith is, and how deep it can go. Most of us who grow up in a religion of self—storage containers, where every idea has a place one can neatly define and lock up if it gets too complicated. But what happens when one sets fire to that storage unit or banana stand? Where does one go when there no more box? How does one know what to do?

This book is about trying to figure out what the next steps are and one's choices on where to go from there after it has come crashing down. This is also a book that asks if American Christianity or evangelicalism is worth saving or reforming. It will not be the same for everyone, and that is okay. Some things I present may be a bit too radical for where you are at, and if we never see eye to eye on this, that is okay too (unless what you believe is actively harming people, that is not okay). All of that to say, I hope what I am about to lay out is helpful to you, wherever you are at in this crazy walk we call faith, and may you find God after the god you left behind.

1

I Still Consider Myself an Evangelical, but Reluctantly

WHEN I WAS 18 and getting ready to graduate high school, I enlisted in the Navy. Thinking I was fulfilling my patriotic duty, I was pretty confident in that decision, until a friend of mine invited me to her church to see how cool their children's ministry operated. I was a theater nerd, and it was a very theatrical set up, so I went and was hooked. Then I sat in on the main service. During it the associate pastor was talking about how we all walk around with this hole in our hearts. He was saying how we try and fill it with everything, jobs, love, money, etc. but it never works. I felt like he was describing me, and then I found out that Jesus was the only thing that can fill that hole and I jumped in headfirst. After all he was describing this deep longing I had to a tee, and it helped that I was terrified of hell. But I spent that summer making great friends, learning about the teachings of Jesus, and volunteering in kid's ministry. It was a lot of fun and I didn't want to leave when it came time to ship off to bootcamp. Being accepted by a community who loved me, and firmly believed that everyone's life would be better if they followed the teachings of Jesus changed mine for the better.

When I think of evangelicalism, this is what I think of, and this is what I have to wrestle with. Something that made me feel warm, fuzzy, and accepted. These relationships were different than any type I had ever encountered in my life. So, the day after the 2016 election I started wondering how this group could turn out like that. My rose tinted glasses, which were already cracked, now shattered. Then I remembered how politically driven some of them were. Abortion being one of the keys as to whether or not the candidate was for or against God.

To be an evangelical means, in the most stripped down and deconstructed way possible, to believe that everyone can benefit from the teachings of Jesus. That is why I consider myself an evangelical to this day. Because of this I believe this vein of Christianity is worth rescuing and the work entailed in that is not easy. In this book I spend a lot of time ripping evangelical Christianity apart and I am not always nice about it. In order to move forward, we must recognize our past. The horrible things we have done, and the sins we have committed along the way. It may be hard to believe but this is not a partisan issue, this is a both and. For the sake of arguing, when someone says they're choosing to follow Jesus, this means they are on the side of life. That means fighting oppression, empire, and injustice wherever people meet it.

If we are to claim on Sunday mornings and believe when we read our bibles that the kin-dom of heaven is at hand, then that means we must be ready to be residents here and now. We pray in the Lord's Prayer, "Your Kingdom come. Your will be done, on earth as it is in heaven." (Matt 6:10 NRSV) Now we forget that to be Christians does not mean we are waiting to get whisked away somewhere, but that our lives have meaning and so do our actions here and now. The current way that American white evangelicalism is practiced is playing into the infamous quote by Karl Marx. It has become the opium of the people because we do nothing but get a hit of that sweet, sweet Jesus opium a few times throughout the week. We have made it into something that is no longer about the here and now, but instead what will be and the dead.

If we agree evangelicalism might be is worth reforming, we must be willing to look at our lives and find out where the dead branches are and prune them. Because of that, this book is meant to be nothing more than a jumping off point. If we don't start somewhere, we will continue to go around in circles aimlessly and in doing so will continue to participate in those systems that keep others in oppression. At the end of the day, we may not all agree on the best way forward but hopefully we can agree that the way things are currently going are not sustainable. The church is so much bigger than we envision it because our daily lives are full of inconveniences. We allow our eyes to stay closed to those around us in need because of the hard areas we refuse to deal with. But we can no longer live this way.

A number of years ago I went through deconstruction of my faith, and it was spectacular. Accepting the things, I do not know has allowed me to freely chase God wherever I found God. While I have been a fan of ancient Judaism, and Jewish writings since I began my walk in Christianity, I have found a lot of the ideas offered in it very helpful. Looking at the larger pool where Christianity is born out of puts into perspective the direction of evangelicalism should go in the future. Because of this I spend a lot of time talking about ancient Judaism and the impact it can have on how God is viewed.

We will also discuss how we have participated in racism, sexism, ableism, and oppression against our lesbian, gay, bisexual, trans, queer, intersex, asexual, and other family members. All of this is necessary to discuss in order to not continue to live in the mistakes of our past. Evangelicals are so quick to discuss the biblical aspects of these issues but neglect the biblical text and narrative as a whole. We want easy answers to complex questions and situations that fit our current social and political standings, but that is not how this goes. Our faith is deep enough, and our God is big enough to live in these complexities.

Sometimes, we forget that Jesus had more faith in us than we do. We are aware of all the miracles he performed, and the wonders he did, but somehow forget he said in John 14:12–14 (NIV),

"Very truly I tell you, whoever believes in me will do the works I have been doing, and they will do even greater things than these, because I am going to the Father. And I will do whatever you ask in my name, so that the Father may be glorified in the Son. You may ask me for anything in my name, and I will do it."

I bring this up not to sound like some naive first year pastor, but that it is easy to forget that Jesus has more faith in us, then we probably do in him, and definitely more than we have in ourselves. I personally find that incredibly comforting. The work of deconstruction can be difficult, but the work of reconstruction is hard work worth doing, especially since both deconstruction and reconstruction are a continuing effort through our lives. It is the active choice to participate in the kin-dom at hand, even on days you don't believe it's here (or exists). Having done the work for the past few years, even on days I don't believe in it, has been more rewarding and honest than when I accepted it blindly and was a good Christian soldier.

I am not writing this book because I am trying to position myself as someone who has all the answers, or as the reconstruction guy. This book has taken over four years to write and has gone through many iterations because that is how reconstruction works. For example, through reading articles and books, listening to podcasts, I had been made aware by how the phrase kingdom of heaven still had a patriarchal ring to it which is why I changed it to the widely accepted kin-dom phrasing (with the exception of scripture quotes). As I was going through the work of rebuilding, I kept searching for jumping off points on how to get restarted because it felt like going at it all head on was too much to handle. As I documented my own process, it made sense to compile it if there were other people trying to do the same thing. Some may find this book an exercise in futility and others may find it helpful.

Evangelical or American Christianity is so small but because of where we find ourselves it has one of the loudest voices in the room which makes it incredibly hard to ignore. When I left it, it felt like there was no place for me. There was nowhere I felt I could lay my head and just learn, which is what this book will hopefully be for those reading it. A brutal place to rip off the bandages so the healing can start. Personally, I spent far too long trying to make my theology fit the framework of whichever church I was in at the time, and it was like putting a piece of tape on a bullet wound. There are so many people who have been looking for next steps, and while I may be arrogant enough to write a book lending my viewpoints, I am not naive enough to believe this is where the work ends. So, either before or after you finish reading this book, please seek out the books listed in Appendix A.

2

"But don't take my word for it, make sure you look it up yourself!" — Your Pastor

I HAVE BEEN TO and worked for several churches where on a Sunday morning, during the sermon, the lead pastor says, don't take my word for it, make sure you look this up yourself! I have also been the guy that has said it while teaching many Bible studies. The funny thing about that sentence is I don't think any of us who worked in mainstream evangelical/seeker sensitive churches ever meant it or wanted our people to do that. This may lead people to begin asking questions we don't have answers to, and that's not something a church can afford, especially during a pandemic. After all, we need to keep the lights on, the heat going, and anyone that isn't a lead pastor at their poverty level salary. Now, does that mean church leaders don't want people to know what the text says? Absolutely not, of course we want that, we just don't want people to call us out when we get it wrong.

Not every church is like this, and not every pastor is like this. But early on, I was one of these guys and the truth is, this attitude for me was driven out of insecurity in my faith (as well as Biblical knowledge). Not that I didn't have enough of it, but I fought (and still do fight) impostor syndrome very hard during my time in ministry. As I started to become more comfortable in what I was teaching, reading, and studying, I started caring less about what my co—workers thought and wanted my friends and people I taught to ask more questions. However, the issue around the statement above, is that pastors are not always prepared for the questions, especially if they are different from the hard—theological stances the church holds on to.

For example, let's say you start reading the Torah (the first five books of both the Hebrew and Christian Bibles) and for some reason you start in Leviticus. You may belong to a church where you believe that the Bible is the absolute Word of God, and it is inerrant and infallible. This shouldn't be that much of a stretch since this is the stance a lot of churches in evangelical American Christianity. You realize in Leviticus 19:19 (NRSV) it says, "You shall keep my statutes. You shall not let your animals breed with a different kind; you shall not sow your field with two kinds of seed; nor shall you put on a garment made of two different materials." And you happen to be wearing a shirt that is a poly/cotton blend. Now this may not be the most earth—shattering thing to read, but it brings about a lot of questions, or should. What else is in the Bible that I don't know about that could be wrong? Is wearing my favorite shirt a sin? What other sins of omission am I committing? It is around this time one would probably want to talk to your pastor and get an idea on what to do with this new information. A meeting is set up and you just word vomit everything, and your pastor's face may become that of a ghost, deathly white.

This is because most of evangelicalism has no idea what to do with the Old Testament or as it is also known, the Hebrew Bible. There is no one school of thought in evangelicalism about it, other than generally it's something that is null and void because Jesus came on the scene, and a new covenant was born out of that. If the Old Testament is referenced it is because of how important Genesis 3 is (the fall) or how it all points to Jesus. Very little is mentioned about how the Christian Bible has rearranged the Old Testament compared to the Hebrew Bible. So little is brought up about the Old Testament in evangelical churches that a 2017 study by Logos revealed that out of the top 100 bible verses quoted in church or sermons, less than 10 where from the Old Testament.[1] To take it one step further, the college courses I've taken from Christian universities in for my undergraduate in pastoral whatever from a college that has since changed its name, Old Testament classes were always a brief background so that the way could be pointed to Christ and so we'd have a working knowledge of it. No more, no less.

A quick aside. After discovering and spending time in the Old Testament, reading Jewish theology, studying Second Temple Judaism, my love of the Bible increased. More importantly, my understanding of who Jesus is, what he came to teach, and how to live made me want to be a better person. It was then my time in discipleship that deepened this love and understanding and continues to make me want to understand more. Now, let us get back to the fake situation from before.

As you sit there in anticipation of what your pastor will say, and the color comes back to his face, he starts to tell you that the "Old Testament" doesn't play into life/faith today. Or he'll say that it is a cultural issue for the time and because of that it has nothing to do with faith and life today. This may bring about a whole new set of questions, for example, "Are there any laws or commands in the 'Old Testament' that deal with today?" or "if that's the case why do we follow the Ten Commandments?" There are platitudes of answers to those questions that your pastor may provide. For some of us, those answers quench the fire, and we can move on with our lives. Now the subject of one article of clothing being made from two types of woven fabric is not something we'd worry about but, remember, in this exercise this church teaches that the Bible is the perfect word of God, infallible and inerrant in every way. If that is the case, then surely this isn't something that we can ignore? Let's say you're still worried after that meeting with your pastor and go home unsatisfied. To calm down you return to the very worn and

1. Brannan, *Writing a Systematic Theology*, 67–81.

underlined pages of the New Testament to read some Jesus to clear your mind of God.

You return to the Sermon on the Mount (Matt 5:1–7:27) to read Jesus' greatest hits and run into a little section that reads:

> Do not think that I have come to abolish the Law or the Prophets; I have not come to abolish them but to fulfill them. I tell you the truth, until heaven and earth disappear, not the smallest letter, not the least stroke of a pen, will by any means disappear from the Law until everything is accomplished. Anyone who breaks one of the least of these commandments and teaches others to do the same will be called least in the kingdom of heaven, but whoever practices and teaches these commands will be called great in the kingdom of heaven. (Matt 5:17–19 NIV)

And a minor or major freak out ensues. Here, you have Jesus telling his followers that they must follow the Law, after all, the heaven and earth have not disappeared! Another meeting is set up and you bring your questions to your pastor again. And again, he tries to reassure you that Jesus came to fulfill the Law, because it was impossible to keep, 613 commands is really tough to do, except for the Perfect One. So, go ahead and ignore all that again and get on with your life.

But this time, for some reason you're more unsettled than the first meeting, and you think to yourself as the Bard put it, there may be something is rotten in the state of Denmark. More questions start to gather as you look deeper into the Bible and start to check what your pastor is teaching. Maybe you take a class at a local college to see what they think of Christianity. You may start to listen to other sermons from different pastors about the same passages that lead you to have a whole new set of questions. You try to talk to your friends or family about this, but they feel you are wading in dangerous territory. They're worried about your faith because you have so many questions, and if fact they question whether you have any faith at all because of them! And now you don't know what to do anymore. This gift that was handed to you, that was once so fit together with a nice bow wrapped on it no longer fits the box it was given in. How does one live with all of this new information and how does it affect one's faith?

There is a small amount of danger that most pastors do not realize they are unleashing when they tell their congregants to look up what they are teaching on. It is something they are, in some cases, not equipped to handle in the mainstream evangelicalism: accountability. Nobody likes being called out on their stuff, especially the guy who is challenging you to do so. Most of us don't know how to handle this humbly, or even rationally. Being able to answer something with, "I don't know" is almost a death sentence in a lot of churches for pastors, especially at a time when attendance is on the decline, and we are all trying to survive. Some double down on scare tactics to keep you going. Others are trying to navigate this new norm of decline and aren't doing that great of a job of it. Because of this, questions that cause you to examine some of the most fundamental aspects of your faith aren't always the most welcome. If you're like me and were on staff at a church when these questions started rearing their heads, it can become an even worse environment. Not only is this your framework for living, but your paycheck is also tied up in this which can cause huge ramifications if you don't toe the party line.

If you have found yourself in any of the situations described and are still reading, then congratulations, you've survived an apocalypse. Contrary to what the History Channel and most end time preachers would have us believe; all apocalypse means is uncovering. That's it. It's not specifically about death, destruction, fire, or brimstone. It's about receiving new knowledge. New knowledge can be scary at first, but if you want a spoiler alert, here's one for you: everything will be alright in the end. As you read about how I've pieced my faith back together it may not be what is right for you and that's okay. Some of the conclusions I come to write here, may change over time after I write them down, and that's okay too. Some already have, after all this book has been four years' worth of work. Faith is an ongoing evolution, and it's a dance. God is ever changing but consistent in some ways. The God of our youth will not be the God of our adulthood, or the God we meet on our deathbed, and that too is okay. I'm partially writing this for reassurance to myself as much as to you. I still struggle with some of this, and probably will for the rest of my days. Some areas we may fundamentally disagree with, and that too will be fine (as long as you are not harming someone with your beliefs), and you can buy me a beer and tell me why I am wrong.

3 _____

Sifting Through the Ashes

IN MATTHEW 7:24–27, JESUS wraps up his sermon by talking about two builders, one who built his house on rock, and the other on sand. I have heard this passage used to describe our faith more times than I can count on my fingers and toes. To generalize it, our faith is like a house, and a strong foundation is needed. Each subject of our theology is like a room in that house, and while we hope deconstruction is just a steady remodel, for most of us. It is sometimes an act of arson and we lit the match, and sometimes dropped it on accident. Deconstruction is a very slippery slope. At the end of it, in the middle of it, we don't know what to do with almost anything we had been given previously. So, in a lot of cases we do nothing, become jaded, think everything is crap, we are just here to procreate, work a meaningless job while the fat cat capitalists get rich off the plight of the proletariat since they do the living and dying. After all religion is just something to keep the dulled masses in line!

When you get together to talk with your friends who are worried about you, you may find merit in a few things from your past, but just because there were one or two good things, that doesn't mean the entire religion thing is good. So, at a party you meet someone new, and you talk with them about how it's not for you anymore and it becomes an hour long whataboutism. What about original sin? Sure, Paul wrote a lot, but what about Peter, he was supposed to be the rock? What about the people who never heard of Jesus? What about the ones who did but said no? And at the end, it may have been a good conversation for both involved. But how do you ask for help if you're the one who is deconstructed? How do we move forward in a world that is familiar but foreign again? Well, sometimes making a list is the easiest way.

I sat for months in this state of realization I was called back into ministry and had no idea what to do with it. I had no idea where to go, or what it looked like. What I did know was I had to move forward in some way, I had sat too long filled with resentment for what had happened and realized I was the one continuing to drink poison and that was no way of living. It took me a while before I was ready to write out my list. I will never forget starting it. I was on my lunchbreak as a Dispatch Manager for an over the road logistics company in the building's café. Throughout that job I had many, many difficult conversations with drivers and scorched my fair share of earth, and I thought, where is God in this? So, on a stained piece of sandwich paper I started writing out things I thought about God. Present, loving, understanding, patient, forgiving, and willing to negotiate. Feeling pretty good about that, I started writing the things that I thought were not worth keeping in my old life. Things that after studying the Bible for a while did not seem to fit, like substitutionary atonement, inerrancy in the Bible, original sin, and so on. After realizing how large these lists could become, I decided to go a different route to try and narrow and sharpen my focus.

To keep with the burnt down house analogy, we need to be like claims adjusters brushing through that rubble. Some of the questions I came up with during this time were the following:

- Is there anything worth saving?
- What parts are structurally sound enough for rebuild?
- What parts can be refurbished?
- What will this cost as far as time and resources?

◻ Is the foundation even worth rebuilding on?

Some of these questions may feel a bit harsh but they are critical to rebuilding. Once you figure out if the foundation you want to lay the groundwork on is worthy of building, then things tend get a bit easier. For example, it may no longer be the God you grew up with but a larger, more mysterious one that isn't defined by a sharp box. We have a habit in evangelical American churches to create an idol out of God and say, this is how it only is or will be. After all, most of us have been taught God is a good father, but if we don't align ourselves with his son Jesus, we will go to hell because of what we did in Genesis 3. So, if one were taught because a person was born into sin, that person would never be good, or they could not be good without a personal relationship with Jesus, which is a lot of baggage to overcome. But realizing that doesn't make sense and is not the character of God laid out over this rich tradition we have, and that there is a lot of unexplored foundation, and there may be more to this is a great way to start. Affirm the good, ditch the toxic. The questions won't end there. Where does prayer life and spirituality fit into all of this? Something that is a bit of a mind screw, especially when trying to put the pieces together is where does authority lay? Is it God? The Bible? The creeds? How will I know I am right?! Spoiler alert: this will be an ongoing struggle, and the answer will be different to most, but we'll get there together, humbly, and hopefully in understanding of one another.

One more thing to consider when it comes to the rebuilding process are resources and time. Books are expensive, and if you're like me and you like to underline and write in them, a library card doesn't really cut it. Also, if you're like me the to read pile is gigantic and daunting at the same time. Reading pop—theology or academic theology is a bit overwhelming. I recommend starting by reading authors that are the opposite of you as possible. James H. Cone is a great place to start; *The Cross and the Lynching Tree* is a must read for white evangelicalism. Also don't forget to rip out Appendix A and take it to your local brick and mortar bookstore. Wherever you end up in this journey will not happen overnight and will take quite a long time. So, consider that when you start this. Try not to get frustrated with the process and in all things take the posture of the student!

Reconstruction is a very time consuming process. Not only are you trying to rebuild something, but there will be setbacks. Things that you may not expect may trip you up or trigger you, and you'll have to put this aside and come back when you're ready. Again, that is okay. Or say for example, that you are married, and you and your spouse are in different stages of this process. One person may not be ready for deconstruction or what you are throwing at them, and while you should let them know where you stand, therefore it is important to find someone to walk through this stuff with. I made the mistake of taking the posture of an arrogant pastor when talking to my spouse about this stuff very early on, forgetting she wasn't in the room or at the table when my mentor and I were having the conversations that started my deconstruction/reconstruction. My pastor posture carried over into the house and I had not realized. At no point was I having a loving conversation with her about the things I had learned. Instead, I was teaching her without her permission. Looking down on her because she had not ascended to my level on academic understanding. What I did not realize at the time was, I was so insecure about these things that my defensiveness and need to be accepted just came off as me being a jerk.

Also, be okay with the fact that there are times where this shifting will become uncomfortable, and you will want to reach back and rely on what you used to believe. Some people double down on bad theology from the past when they're unsure what to do or believe or are feeling overwhelmed. As tough as it is, you must press on and go forward. Whatever it was you left, you left for a reason. Circle back around to the list I recommended making at the beginning and write one down of the reasons why what you had was no longer working for you. I cannot tell you how many times I have reverted to mine, and how that has knocked me out of my funk.

4

Laying Groundwork on the Bible Part 1

THE CHRISTIAN BIBLE IS the official sacred scripture of Christianity, which if you did not know by now, you are welcome. In a religion where a lot of people disagree on many, many things, this is generally accepted. Because of this, the Bible plays a central role in our faith. When I was growing up, though not a regular church member, I *knew* the Bible was the literal word of God. However, I did not know what that meant. During my time studying the text and reading books about the Bible, I had come to learn a lot of information that changed how I viewed the Bible to have been written. During that time, I was a College Ministry Director and was teaching a class where we would go deeper into whatever subjects they wanted to. One week, a woman who attended wanted to know about the formation of the Bible we have now. The research was fascinating, and I realized the number of translations, votes, and fights people went through in order to get the current edition of the New Revised Standard Version and New International Version that I currently use. All this history whether we know it or not informs how we read it.

When I was in undergrad at the University of Toledo the first time I went there, I had the honor of sitting at the feet of Dr. James Waddell. If you ever have that opportunity or he is lecturing near you, make the trip. It will be worth it. He taught my class Old Testament class, which was about its formation, the surrounding Near Eastern culture, and a bit of its history. This class blew my mind open and fundamentally changed some of my views on God and the Bible and helped shaped a lot of my New Testament views as well. In class we discussed the various creation stories around that time (Tiamat, Epic of Gilgamesh, etc.) and how all of that may have played into the formation. What I am about to cover is a crash course on what we covered there, what I've learned since then, and why how we view how God interacts with creation at the beginning of our Bible should affect how we view our relationship with God (and subsequently Jesus). Hopefully, retooling this little bit will help.

Julius Wellhausen was a German biblical scholar and teacher who lived from the mid—nineteenth century through the early twentieth century. He had led a group of scholars to try and discover who would have actually written down Torah. Until a certain point, the Israelite tradition had been an oral one passed down from one generation to the next. However, at some point, somebody decided to write it all down. The question was, who decided to do this? Through their research, this group came up with something known as the Documentary Hypothesis.[1] What this boiled down to is that the Pentateuch (Greek translation of the first five books of the Hebrew and Christian Bibles), "was derived from originally independent, parallel and complete narratives, which were subsequently combined into the current form by a series of redactors (editors)."[2] What does this mean? Well, four groups came together to create one narrative that was derived from the teachings of Moses on Mount Sinai.

1. Hinson, *Documentary Hypothesis*, 1.
2. Hinson, *Documentary Hypothesis*, 2.

GROUP ONE: JEHOIVIST/YAHWIST SOURCE (J).

This group uses the term Yahweh for the name of God, and focuses mainly on, "most of the Primeval History, the Ancestral Saga, the escape to Egypt and travel to Sinai, God's appearance to Moses at Sinai and the revelation of a law code, and some of the narratives of wilderness wanderings in Numbers." [3] So, J is considered the sources for the majority of Genesis, Exodus, and Numbers and it was believed to have been written around 950 BC in Judah. [4]

GROUP TWO: ELOHIM SOURCE (E).

The writer referred to God as Elohim, which is less personal and more generic than Yahweh, also had an account similar to J about the Ancestral Saga but focused more on the prophetic leadership relating to Abraham, Jacob, Joseph, and Moses; named the mountain Moses received Torah from Mount Herob, and uses the term, fear of God. This was thought to have been written in Israel around 850 BC. [5]

GROUP THREE: DEUTERONOMIST SOURCE (D)

This group is thought to have edited Torah and combined the J and E source together while adding their own source, Deuteronomy, which focuses on the monotheistic nature that, "Israel worshiping one God in one place God chooses." [6] This was believed to have been written in 600 BC in Jerusalem during the religious reforms under Josiah. [7]

---

3. Hinson, *Documentary Hypothesis*, 3.

4. Hinson, *Documentary Hypothesis*, 3.

5. Hinson, *Documentary Hypothesis*, 4.

6. Hinson, *Documentary Hypothesis*, 5.

7. Hinson, *Documentary Hypothesis*, 5.

GROUP FOUR: PRIESTLY SOURCE (P)

This was thought to have been a separate source to maintain the Israelite identity while in exile outside of Jerusalem. It's thought that this was a complete document that was woven into Genesis, Exodus, and Numbers, and believed that the priestly source also contributed solely to Leviticus. Things like detailed information on circumcision, the dietary laws, building of the tabernacle came from this. Finally, this section was believed to have been written in sixth century BCE during the Babylonian exile, then sometime within the fifth century BCE all four sources were combined and edited to be the Torah that we have today.[8]

It would be inappropriate if I did not bring up that not all scholars currently view Documentary Hypothesis as the gold standard. Until the 1970s, most biblical scholars accepted Wellhausen's Documentary Hypothesis on how the Torah was formed. However, a biblical scholar named John Van Seters published a booked in 1975 called *Abraham in History and Tradition*, and other biblical scholars around this time published works questioning parts of Wellhausen's work. However, when I was introduced to Documentary Hypothesis, it served as an introduction and jumping off point. Part of my deconstruction and reconstruction was trying to figure out where the Bible landed, and how it got to be what it is today. The idea that the Bible was whispered into someone's ear by God as they wrote it down never really worked for me, and as I grew, I realized I did not understand what I meant when I thought it was the literal word of God. When that fell apart, I wasn't sure why the Bible could even be trustworthy. However, after learning that my tradition is born out of a much richer tapestry and communal gathering that figured out together how they understand God through their experience, and how God continued to show up after that, made this more tangible sense. So, if you find this subject as interesting as I do, there is a world of reading ahead of you.

8. Hinson, *Documentary Hypothesis*, 6.

Moses has always been attributed to writing the Torah. When we discover that the formation of Torah does not come from just one source, but many can be a bit overwhelming, especially if that has been the worldview you've been working from. After all there are passages that state Moses wrote it (Exod 34:27; Deut. 31:22; Mark 12:26; John 1:17). And after being taught, if we don't take the Bible as inerrant or infallible, it throws everything into question. How can we trust it? This is whether or not you take the seven days of creation as literal argument, and as I have been told, if you don't believe it, you might as well throw the entire Bible out and ignore it. I think that argument may not hold as much water as originally thought. With all that in mind, let's talk about everyone's favorite Apostle, Paul.

Not everyone believes Paul wrote all the letters attributed to him. While there is some disagreement in this area, here's what most scholars agree on him writing: Philemon, Romans, First Corinthians, Second Corinthians, Philippians, First Thessalonians, and Galatians. The letters where the split is 50/50 on whether Paul wrote them are Second Thessalonians and Colossians. While they sound a lot like Paul, the dating is hard to figure out, but again, this is a 50/50. The remaining letters: Ephesians, First Timothy, Second Timothy, and Titus were most likely written out of the "Pauline School," which a group of people that were discipled by someone who would have been discipled by Paul. They would have intimately known the letters and most likely wrote them to adapt to changing times and theology.[9] [10]What does this mean for Paul's letters and why are they in the Bible?

Let me tell you about a little tool called, pseudepigrapha, also known as the act of falsely attributing someone's name to something they didn't write. It is an important part of reconstruction, especially if you are trying to figure out what to do with the Bible as a whole. In my experience, when it comes to deconstruction, people are afraid of it when focusing on the Bible because the question of where authority lies comes up repeatedly. Learning

9. Concannon, *Paul and Authorship*, lines 1–38.

10. Just, *Deutero-Pauline Letters,* lines 1–60.

about this subject, however, put things in new light for me and was very freeing to my reconstruction. Honestly, it redeemed Paul to me, which is no easy task. Pseudepigraphy was practiced between 200 BC to 200 AD and one of the ways it can be described is, it is written in the style of the intended author. When this was being practiced, this was not uncommon in the ancient world. Something that is hard to remember is, during this time, the focus on historical accuracy wasn't as intense as it is today unless it was a library that was trying to get copies of original manuscripts; things were written over a longer period of time with more than one author in the process of it.

As I was finishing up the final manuscript of this book, I became aware of Bart D. Ehrman and his book *Jesus, Interrupted.* I highly recommend reading this book, the depth that it dives into for this subject is immense and is something everyone should read. To pull from his writings on it would do the subject injustice, so please check it out. However, getting back to the subject at hand. Paul's letters are canonical because they're important to the overarching narrative, and this is coming from someone who isn't particularly impressed by Paul (even less impressed with the people that treat him as Messiah).

When we look at the Bible, we often overlook how much oral tradition plays into it, and that more often than not, it was written down way after the fact. This is the story of the synoptic Gospels and most of the New Testament. What does this have to do with JEDP, and why examining the first bit of Genesis and how those effects how we see God, and how we set up a relationship with God? Well, oral tradition was very much alive and well in ancient Israel, and this honestly was/is not a bad thing. There are these four traditions (JEDP) that all find themselves together in the same place at the same time. It is believed during this time, they saw all of this, and a group of redactors assembled them together, to create the Torah.[11] Traditions that where orally handed down to one another, were then written down, all attributed to Moses that followed them back into exile. Missing pieces of a puzzle that

11. Hinson, *Documentary Hypothesis,* pg. 7.

finally became whole. This assembled book shaped Judaism, and by association Christianity. Now to be clear, there is plenty written about the formation of the Hebrew and Christian Bible, and this is a drop in the bucket. There are more amazing books out there that go into deeper depth than I have, but all of this is preamble for what I am about to get into, and I feel it is very important to make sense of what is to come.

In the next chapter we will be diving into the Babylonian exile, getting into their gods, formation of Torah as story, and starting to reveal why all of this matters more than we ever may have realized.

5

Laying Groundwork on the Bible Part 2

I LOVE GENESIS. I'M more of a Phil Collins than Peter Gabriel fan unlike a former teacher of mine (sorry Barry). The thing I love about them, is there are two very distinct, but similar sounds to them. It's like reading Genesis 1 and then chapter 2. It is almost the exact same thing, yet different at the same time.

While the Israelites are being inundated with Babylonian culture and way of life, they are trying to reassess who they are, and how they can maintain their identity in exile. They haven't had to do this since they had been given the traditions by Moses, and now they're all assembled for the first time trying to make this work in one place. So, how does one maintain a monotheistic culture in a polytheistic society? After all, according to their tradition, they will not have another god before their God (Exod 20:3). Something I think is really interesting to say here: YHWH isn't saying at Sinai that there aren't other gods. YHWH at this moment in time is saying not to put those other gods before YHWH.

In Genesis 1, we see the creation of the heavens and earth as God's spirit hovers over the chaos and water:

- Day one, the light is created, and darkness is separated from the light.

- Day two, the waters below are separated from the waters above by sky.

- Day three, land and vegetation are created.

- Day four, the sun, the moon, and the stars are created.

- Day five, we see the skies and seas filled up with fish and birds.

- Day six, creatures for the land are created and God says let us create man in our image.

- Day seven, Sabbath.

In almost every church I have attended or worked at, the leading explanation of the "us" or "our" is that it's the trinity at work. I'd like to offer up a different idea, or rather, a different interpretation using some imagery and citing another source later on in the Bible that I believe is consistent with what's going on here.

Imagery is a large thing in the Bible and typically evangelicalism all but ignores. Trying to learn it after a lifetime of ignoring it is, for me personally, a pain. One time, while sitting down with my Evangebros cohost Don, he and I were talking about the plagues that were released onto the Egyptians. Something Don had brought up to me that I was completely unaware of, was that the imagery associated with each plague was the defeat of a specific Egyptian god. For example, the god of the Nile, Hapi, was defeated when the Nile turned to blood.

The act of weaving regional gods into the Hebrew Bible is something practiced through imagery, and I think that is what is happening in Genesis 1. This idea is something brought to light to me by, again, my Old Testament teacher Dr. Waddell. In that class, he brought up the heavenly court YHWH seems to head up, about creating man. The idea being that the other gods did exist, but that YHWH was the head of all. In this idea, YHWH would have been responsible for creating the Babylonian gods. Let's look at the days of creation again, and the opening to the Enuma Elish, the Babylonian creation story.

The Enuma Elish is one of the oldest creations stories and predates the Hebraic creation story. The creation story at the beginning of the Bible was heavily influenced by others in that region at the time. For example, here are the opening lines to the Babylonian story, "When the heavens above did not exist, and earth beneath had not come into being — there was Apsû, the first in order, their begetter, and demiurge Tia—mat, who gave birth to them all; they had mingled their waters together"[1]

An article written by Joshua J. Mark for Ancient History Encyclopedia titled, "*Enuma Elish-The Babylonian Epic of Creation-Full Text*" I found to be most helpful when looking at some of the summarization of the *Enuma Elish*, given the direction I am going with this. Mark summarizes the opening as such, "In the beginning, there was only undifferentiated water swirling in chaos. Out of this swirl, the waters divided into sweet, fresh water, known as the god Apsu, and salty bitter water, the goddess Tiamat. Once differentiated, the union of these two entities gave birth to the younger gods."[2]

In Genesis 1 we have YHWH hovering over the mixed waters Apsu and Tiamat. On the second day, YHWH separates the waters below (Tiamat) via the sky, also known as the Babylonian god Anshar (god of sky under the clouds), from the waters above (Apsu). On the third day we see land (Antum goddess of earth) and vegetation (Aruru is the nature goddess) are created. The fourth day brought the sun (Adramelech sun god), the moon (Sin moon god), and the stars (Igigi god of the heavens above the clouds/collective name for the gods above the clouds).[3] Then day five and six are the creation of the creatures for air, land, and sea, while we see YHWH speaking with the divine council.

Why does this matter? Well, one way of interpreting this can be as an early act of subversion. The Babylonians would have recognized the beginning of Genesis, and at time when you are defeated in battle, and brought into a foreign land, you would have abandoned your god and taken up the worship of that foreign god.

1. Mark, *Enuma Elish,* lines 108–112.

2. Mark, *Enuma Elish,* lines 19–22.

3. Mark, *Mesopotamian Pantheon,* 44–47, 52, 58–63, 93, 94, 262, 263, 562–564, & 577–581.

Here, we see the Israelites subvert that, and worship in a monotheistic fashion by incorporating Babylonian gods as the lesser and putting YHWH above them. So, what does this have to do about how factors into how we interact with God? Everything.

A nation of people are gathered in the same area all together for what is most likely the first time since the exodus from Egypt and what do they do? Come together and make sense of what they were given from Moses. They weave in a creation story within their creation poem/narrative to show their captors that while they have no choice but to accept the yoke they have been given; it will not stop them from being who they are. It does not stop you from being who you are created to be. It gives off a "oh captors, you think you're so great. Our God tamed the waters and chaos that you believe to be your gods. Our God created the things you worship. Our God loved us into being. So, give us your best shot, we'll take it, but it doesn't stop who we are and what we will do" sort of vibe. Our creation narrative is birthed out of subversion. Torah is birthed out of subversion. Jesus is subversion in the flesh. Christianity at its best continues in this tradition that is about rejecting of what is going on in the surrounding region and cultural norms for something new, progressive, and it has been this way since it's salad days. So that says a lot about the people, but what does that say about our God?

6

The God of Creation, Destruction, and Recreation

AS A YOUNG EVANGELICAL, I was taught that all I needed to know about who God is was found in the Bible. When I started to read the Bible was when I started my journey towards deconstruction, especially when I started reading about ancient Judaism. Learning about what was going on and being written about during the time Jesus was alive and teaching reformed my faith in a way I could never had expected. The Bible went from a dead book to a living story. Part of putting the pieces of my faith back together meant I had to look at the foundational things I believed about God. During my early years of evangelical Christianity, I had read the Bible backwards. Revelation to Genesis seemed to be the way everyone I knew read it. The idea being we knew how the story ended; who cared about how it started? When reconstruction and rebuilding became very real, I decided to start in the beginning and try to imagine what God was doing from the start. This approach not only changed how I view God but also gave Jesus more nuance and realism. It helped me to care about the things I believe God cares about.

Most denominations of Christianity are familiar with a lectionary: a calendar of passages from the Bible that are broken down weekly that are covered over a series of time to help guide worship and teaching schedules. Judaism has something similar, called Portions. This is similar, but it's a grouping centering on the Torah instead of the Gospels. So, what I'd like to do is focus the first bit of portions instead of breaking down by chapter (although there are parts I will break down chapter to chapter). Most of what I am about to go over was born out of the Torah portions episodes of my podcast Evangebros, and the conversations with my friend Don. During this series we also followed the website Aleph Beta which is a Jewish site that discusses the Torah portions. I highly recommend getting a subscription to them if you are able. As we go over the first four portions in the reading cycle, I wanted to split them up. The first two focus heavily on storytelling, as in, it probably did not physically happen, but it is still important because of what was going on in the world and the foundation for Israel's story. The ordering of the gods below YHWH, and how these creation narratives continually find their way throughout the Hebrew and Christian Bible. So, get your Bible, and let's get into this!

PORTION ONE: B'REISHEET (GEN 1:1-6:8).

There is a lot to cover in this portion, so strap in. Chapter 1, God creating the heavens and earth, while establishing Godself above all gods and creating humankind. Chapter 2, God plants a garden and places it in the east and it is named Eden. Adam is placed there by God after he was already created in order for him to work and to care for it. The first time something is named as not being good is that Adam is alone. Therefore, Eve is created from Adam as an equal partner to share in the struggles with him. They were both naked and felt no shame. So far, we have God as a character that wants to share in creation, by continuing to create. God recognizes, not Adam, that the isolation isn't good therefore as an act of compassion and to complete creation, Eve is brought into being. So far as the humans are concerned, there is no real emotion, or at least no emotion conveyed yet in the text.

In Chapter 3, the serpent points out that the one tree currently denied to Adam and Eve, the tree of knowledge of good and evil, will allow them to become more like God, so Eve consumes the fruit. She saw it was good for food, pleasing, and good for gaining wisdom, so she and Adam ate of the fruit. Their eyes are opened, and they realized they were naked, so they made clothes for themselves and hid as they heard God walking through the garden. God is concerned for them and asks where they are. When Adam answers with the, I heard you in the garden, and I was afraid because I was naked, so, I hid line. Let's think about that for a second. Until this point, no emotion has been shown from Adam or Eve, and after the fruit is consumed there is shame followed directly by fear. Their first step into becoming more like God is to feel shame. That is a powerful image. Growing up, for me, God was always portrayed as this powerful, all knowing, omnipresent being. Never once had I thought of God feeling shame. This is something we will touch on in the next portion, so please keep this in mind.

And what happens when they give God this answer? God's response is not to condemn them. God responds with a question: "who told you that you were naked? Have you eaten from the tree of which I commanded you not to eat?" (Gen 3:11, NRSV). God does not show anger toward Adam and Eve. God addresses the shameful issue at hand. God's first reaction from this revelation is to go directly to the serpent and dole out a punishment for the action. Then the punishment is handed down to Eve, and finally Adam. At no point does God make any statement to imply humanity is broken or separated from God due to this action. There are consequences, but separation from God is not named as one of them. The earth has changed, there is increased pain in childbirth. This is fun because that could mean Eve may have known more subdued pains of childbirth before she left the garden. There are also traditions that maintain Cain was born into the garden. Then we see that while Adam must still till the soil and work the grounds, it will become difficult, and at some point, he will return to the dust from which he was formed.

While the concept of Original Sin has been around for most of church history, the way we currently understand it is generally attributed to Augustine of Hippo, and it is the idea that everyone who is born is born sinful. From birth, people are born with the urge to disobey God in every shape and way possible. After all, as most of us learned in Sunday School, this is the reason why Jesus died on the cross. This concept is not only good for trying to explain away the urges that one gets from time to time to do something "bad" but is also very helpful when you are trying to control a large number of people. At the time this idea originated, God was the answer for everything, and the church imprisoned scientists for claiming the Sun was the center of the universe. If you are in a position of power and you are trying to maintain the power structure, it is easier to tell people they are broken and sinful, and the only way to salvation is the one you offer. Most Christians do not realize the doctrine of Original Sin does not exist in Judaism. Considering our tradition is born out of theirs, our ideas of sins should stem from there. What does it say about a people who think no matter what they do, they will never be good enough for their creator? Imagine growing up knowing there is nothing keeping you from God's love, and that you are good from the day of your birth.

After that, God continues to address the trauma of the situation by making clothes for them. Before sending them out into the world, God continues to ensure they are protected and safe from what was inflicted by cutting, sewing, and hemming garments for both of them. Then they are walked out to work the ground, "from which he had been taken" (Gen 3:23, NRSV) meaning, Adam is familiar with his surroundings. He is going back to familiar territory, to continue the work he was doing in Eden. Things have changed but remain the same, like going home after your first time living away.

In chapter 4, Cain murders Able which leads God to ask Cain where Able is. Again, if there is a separation between us and God, one would think that after freshly murdering someone, God would not only not ignore them, but also could not be in their presence. Yet here is God talking to and being present with Cain. We find out the bloods of Abel are crying out from the ground to God (and yes, the Hebrew intends for it to be pluralized, as in Able and his descendants are crying out). And yet again, God addresses the trauma of the situation. God asks Cain knowing full well what happened, and when Cain doesn't fess up, a punishment for the reaction of killing this brother is set forth. After all, Cain had no experience with human death yet. Because of this, some traditions say Cain's punishment was too severe and God was at fault for what happened, because God did not intervene until after the act had occurred. In that case, the blood isn't crying for justice for Cain, but because of the neglect by God.[1] This idea is so foreign to the American evangelical Christian narrative I was brought up on. The idea that God is not being fair is something we will touch back on, and it is worth noting.

At the end of the day, to prevent more bloodshed, this time inflicted upon Cain, God protects him by casting a mark upon him so everyone will know not to kill him. To be clear, God is protecting a murderer, in order to stop more bloodshed from occurring. This should cause pause to absorb the compassion of this God. We also see the birth of Seth, who is the first person born in the image of man and not God (Gen 5:3). In chapter 5 we see the genealogy from Adam to Noah (and including Enoch who didn't die but walked with God, whatever that means).

From here, in chapter 6 we get a rather heartbreaking insight into the character of God. Right before this first set of portions end, we get these two verses, "And the LORD was sorry that he had made humankind on earth, and it grieved him to his heart. So the LORD said, 'I will blot out from the earth the human beings I have created—people together with animals and creeping things and birds of the air, for I am sorry that I have made them" (Gen 6:5–7, NRSV).

This is incredibly striking and should again cause us to pause at the weight of the emotions on display. After all, this is the same God who took time to care for Adam and Eve before they were

---

1. Greenwald, *Your Brother's Blood*, lines 11–15.

led out of the garden. This is the same God who told them to be fruitful and multiply the earth. What happened to the God who addressed the trauma of that situation? Most have been taught to read these verses as if they portray an angry, spiteful, vengeful God, ready to strike down anyone. I am not sure I agree with that assessment.

What we see is God showing similar emotions to what Adam and Eve displayed. There is shame in this. Shame that implies, this action I committed caused more death and destruction. After all, this is the same God who tried to avoid more bloodshed by protecting Cain from death! Here is a God full of emotion, and how often have we been denied showing emotion because of the communities we were a part of?

At one point I during a conversation with Don, I said these verses show God having very human emotions, showing regret. I said that I imagine in a parent's worst moments of frustration, they may regret bringing that child into existence, and that seems to be on display here. Don responded with a question that honestly shook me a bit: "Is it when we have regret, we have human emotions, or when we have regret, we have God—like emotions?"[2] This opened my mind to thinking again about the garden scene. In the moment after eating the fruit, Adam and Eve exhibit shame, and regret and shame go hand in hand. They are exhibiting God—like emotions since we've yet to see them display any at all. This is an interesting take on God, after all, most evangelical teachings I've heard say that in order for God to save humanity and to experience human emotion, God had to come in the form of Jesus. But the text does not seem to show that to be the case. Here we see a God brokenhearted over the creation that was brought into being, that was good, but no longer is.

2. Evangebros, *Breisheet*, October 2018.

PART TWO: NOAH (GEN 6:9-11:32)

Chapter 6, verse 9, the text introduced Noah, who was a righteous and blameless man among the people in his time, but considering what is about to happen, that may not be saying much. Maybe he just sucked the least out of this version of humanity. And this is something that should again give us pause. God is chasing someone who is, by the standards of his generation, not the worst. It doesn't mean he wasn't terrible. There is a lot of time dedicated to work on this huge ark, and not one sentence is devoted to Noah spreading the word about the oncoming flood, there is no plea from Noah on behalf of the people to God to try and delay it, change it, or not send it at all.[3] So, after the instructions are given to build the ark, Noah keeps to himself, waits until the last minute to get on the ark with his family, and makes no offer to friends. Beyond that, we have to struggle with, whether God is committing genocide because we believe in this story as somewhat literal, or it is a story/parable and God going through the process of uncreating. I personally read this as storytelling and will present the following as such.

God is removing the separation between the waters above and below, removing the breath of life from humanity, and drowning the livestock. Even in verse 7:22, we see everything on land which "had the breath of life in its nostrils died," (NRSV) which is a very intentional and peculiar way of saying that. After all, the last time we see this phrase is when the narrator of Genesis says in 2:7 that God had formed mankind from the dust, "and breathed into his nostrils the breath of life; and the man became a living being" (NRSV). God is uncreating. God is removing God's spirit from the earth. For the second time, we have a God over the chaos and waters.

This is even more evident after the flood waters have subsided, and we see the use of a dove. After seven days, a dove returns with an olive branch to Noah. The dove is seen throughout the text as an image of God (think Matthew's version of the baptism of

3. Evangebros, *Noach*, October 2018.

Jesus), so one can argue the Spirit is returning to this new creation. Noah and his family are led out of the ark by God and are told to be fruitful and multiply. Again, we have this new Adam and Eve imagery, and for the first time in the text, humans are given permission to eat the animals. God also establishes a new covenant with humanity in the form of a rainbow, promising we will never be flooded in this way again. From this new creation, humanity is birthed and spread throughout the world until the Tower of Babel in chapter 11.

Babel is interesting because there are people working together, creating bricks, trying to reach the heavens. And then you have God and the heavenly hosts/council that are barely paying attention. To paraphrase Don, God is using binoculars to see what they're doing and ends up coming down to take a look at everything. Seeing what they are up to, God decides to confuse the language of everyone, and they scatter across the earth. The reason we're given for this is, God saying that nothing would be impossible for humankind, so the language is changed. I tend to lean into the camp that says God is already familiar with this scene.

Perhaps pre-flood habits were starting to form, and God decided to go a different route this time thanks to the covenant God made with Noah. It should also be stated here that Babel is Babylon, also known as where the Israelites will be exiled, where they will form the Torah. After the great scattering, we see another genealogy end with a man named Terah who took his son Abram, daughter-in-law Sarai, and grandson Lot to go live in Canaan. But they decided to settle in Harran where Terah would eventually die.

To summarize the first two portions so far, God had created everything out of the chaos, from the smallest seed to the gods that are worshiped by others. When humankind was created, they opted to take the role of judge from God by finding out for themselves what is good and what is evil instead of waiting to be taught. This led to God finding out what happened, addressing the trauma and shame of the situation while still teaching that there are consequences to actions: increased birthing pains, and working the soil harder than ever, total separation from God is not listed as a punishment.

After all, Cain kills his brother and is still protected by God. These consequences land creation in a dire place, and God decides to recreate the world by finding the least crappy person to be the new Adam, and after seeing God remove God's spirit from earth for the destruction, we see it brought back with the dove and olive branch. After deciding to never do this again, God creates the covenant with Noah using the rainbow. Then seeing humanity come together to build the tower of Babel, and perhaps starting to get back to some old habits, God decides to mess with their language, and they disband.

Part of why I love Genesis is because God is still forming who God is going to be. God has changed a lot and reacts differently in these first few portions. Beginning as a creator that has compassion as God hand sews garments so Adam and Eve will be protected. Then God continues down the compassionate route and decided to spare Cain after he murders his brother. Yet as time goes on, we can argue God is filled with great shame seeing the state of humanity and no longer cares to protect them but instead start fresh with Noah and his family. Things may seem rocky but, Abram has arrived, and the world will not be the same.

7

The God of Abraham and You!

THE NEXT TWO PORTIONS differ from the previous two, mainly because almost every major civilization of the ancient Near East we have record of, has a creation story and flood story. What starts to set apart ancient Israel is how they latched on to monotheism, the worship of one god, instead of continuing to practice polytheism, the worship of multiple gods, like their neighbors. With Abraham we receive the first patriarch and the covenant from God promising that the descendants of Abraham are to be a blessing to all nations. This diverges from what was common in the world at the time where there is now a global God who wasn't defined by regions and decided to get back into some type of relationship with humanity.

When I was first starting to read Genesis while learning about ancient Judaism, I realized that as an evangelical, I had never focused on the type of person the Bible describes Abraham to be. To me he was always the guy who was willing to go further than anyone today because of his faith. After all God told him to kill his son, and it was Abraham's faith that brought him to do that. When I was writing my first prayer meeting many years ago, I planned to focus on the binding of Isaac, illustrating how faith was the most important thing we have and how we should be willing to do whatever God called us to, no matter what the cost.

I was a bit radical. However, after reading what some of the rabbis had written about him, and reading what the Bible said versus what I had been told, and wrestling through this with my friend Don changed my life. Abraham went from what I previously described to the champion of justice and hospitality, which made Jesus's life and ministry more attainable. Because of what Abraham did, it removed this fake veil of pedestal Jesus where I could never be like him because he's the son of God. For example, growing up in my faith, I was taught that we should try and imitate Jesus, but because of our sinful nature I would never be able to actually act like him. I would always fall short (don't worry, we will address this concept later on). With Abraham however, here was a biblical character that I could act like. Someone I had been given no frame of reference for other than his great faith. Suddenly there was an example on how to live without feeling imitating Jesus was far away. I can make food for people; I can defend people by trying to find some type of compromise. Faith became tangible and reachable in a way it hadn't been for me previously.

PORTION THREE: LECH LECHA (GEN 12:1-17:27)

There has been so much work done on Abram (later Abraham) and there is no way I will begin to scratch the surface on him and his relationship with God. That being said, what I am about to present is such a small fraction of what is available to you, and if you decide to go down this rabbit hole, I cannot state how worth it, it is.

After whom knows how long, God decides to rejoin into community with humanity, mainly by calling Abram to something more. Genesis 12:1b-3 says, "go from your country, your people and your father's household to the land that I will show you. I will make you into a great nation, and I will bless you; I will make your name great, and you will be a blessing. I will bless those who bless you, and whoever curses you I will curse; and all the peoples on earth will be blessed through you" (NIV).

Abram is called by God to leave and to continue the journey they had originally set out on, so he and his companions leave with all of their possessions to head out to Canaan. While on the path, Abram builds two separate altars, one in Shechem where God tells Abram that his offspring will inherit the land, and the other outside of Bethel. During their sojourning, a famine happens, and Abram, Sarai, and Lot must go to Egypt. This is the start of a pattern we see in the text, after all, Jacob, Abram's grandson, and his family sojourn there during a great famine as well. When they arrive, Abram, who already knows that God is going to make a great nation of him, thinks it is best for Sarai to act as his sister, so he isn't killed. Pharaoh takes a liking to her, and when she goes into his palace, Abram receives, "sheep and cattle, male and female donkeys, male and female servants, and camels" (Gen 12:16, NIV).

You did read that correctly: Abram receives human beings—slaves—while he is there. This isn't something that should be glossed over. Slavery is/was a real thing when the text was written, and it is something that is still going on today. It is wrong, it is an abomination, and it is something we must recognize when we see it in the text. Even though this was written in a time and place where slavery was common, and even though it is something that the overarching narrative of the Hebrew and Christian Bibles fight against in all forms. This doesn't mean we should not struggle through this part and recognize what is happening.

God then sends an unnamed plague onto Pharaoh and his household. When it is discovered that Sarai is Abram's wife and not sister, Pharaoh freaks out and sends them packing with all they have. This brings them back to where they were, to Bethel, at the altar Abram had set up previously. Because of how much Abram and Lot had accumulated, the land couldn't support their camps. In other words, there was not enough food or water for the cattle and people, and there had to have been infighting amongst their servants on what belonged to whom, so Abram decided to split them up. He asks Lot where he would like to go and gives him the first choice of the land. Lot decides to encamp in Jordan toward Zoar because it was, "well watered, like the garden of the LORD" (Gen 13:10, NIV). The text goes on to say in verses 12 and 13 of the NIV translation, "So Lot chose for himself the whole plain of the Jordan and set out toward the east. The two men parted company: Abram lived in the land of Canaan, while Lot lived among the cities of the plain and pitched his tents near Sodom. Now the people of Sodom were wicked and were sinning greatly against the Lord."

So, Lot decides to go live near Sodom, a place where the people were wicked and sinning greatly against God, but the area was well watered and like the garden of the LORD—a place that resembled Eden. How could a place with the same resources as Eden (which was created as good by God) be a place where people that are wicked? What does it even mean to be wicked in this context? Well, we'll get there. But for now, Abram parted ways and went to sojourn in Canaan, where God tells Abram that Canaan will be the land that his descendants will eventually inherit. While doing this, God reaffirms the covenant God made with Abram, and Abram travels to Hebron and builds another altar to the LORD.

As some rulers are prone to do, a pissing contest forces the kings of the region to battle. When things were looking dire, the kings of Sodom and Gomorrah fled, and their cities were sacked and carried off, and because Lot had taken up residence around Sodom, he was taken too. Luckily for Lot, a captured man escaped and made his way to Abram. Then Abram takes on the persona of Liam Neeson in *Taken*. After everyone is liberated, we are introduced to someone who is often ignored in most circles I have run with, because Christians have no idea what to do with this character beyond the brief explanation, we see in Hebrews 7. Meet Melchizedek, king of Salem! "Then Melchizedek king of Salem brought out bread and wine. He was priest of God Most High, and he blessed Abram, saying, 'Blessed be Abram by God Most High, Creator of heaven and earth. And praise be to God Most High, who delivered your enemies into your hand.' Then Abram gave him a tenth of everything" (Gen 14:18–20, NIV).

Something that is important whenever reading the Hebrew Scriptures is to not read the New Testament into it. In my experience Christians are often taught to read the Bible backwards, starting with maybe the Gospels, most likely Paul depending on who your teacher is, then Revelation, and if you want, go ahead, and read the Hebrew Scriptures. However, with any book it is always best to start at the beginning, especially when the narrative builds upon what was written before. When this part of the text was written, the New Testament obviously had not happened yet, so we must honor how the original readers may have read it. It helps us moving forward, as part of that story. For example, a lot of Christians have interpreted Melchizedek as Jesus, as recognized by Abram, which is why there was bread and wine to serve as the Eucharist). Also, Abram paid him a tithe of what he had, prior to giving everything back to the kings who gathered there.

Psalm 110, according to David, the LORD has made him forever a priest in the order of Melchizedek. Hebrews 7 goes into great length about Jesus and Melchizedek. But is that really what is going on here? I tend to be in the camp that says, no, that is not in fact what is happening. Think about how much baggage we are already bringing to the text when we read through Genesis for the first time. We have been inundated with so much information about the Melchizedek archetype that when we read his name it ends up being a call forward to what has been written. So, that being said, is all of that what's really going here?

I think no, it is much simpler and potentially a little uncomfortable for some of us. Melchizedek, king of Salem, is someone who serves YHWH, the same God that Abram serves, and Abram recognizes this. This is an example of God exposing God's self to someone in a different land. Instead of trying to evangelize, Abram recognizes what Melchizedek represents and pays respect to it. Then, he moves on. We don't know how to deal with this as evangelicals, because we are trained from a young age to save everyone, in some cases even if their version of God is just slightly different from ours.

From here, Abram returns everything that was looted, and the king of Sodom tells Abram he can keep everything but the people. Abram's reaction is very important to what happens later in the text: He refuses anything from the king and responds by saying he had sworn an oath to God to never accept anything from him as to not give him the opportunity to boast and say the king of Sodom made Abram rich. Why is this important? Well, remember how Sodom was described: Sodom is anti—everything God is.

We have now arrived at Genesis chapter 15, one of the most important but most overlooked chapters of the Bible, especially within the evangelical American church. Over the years I have come to believe this chapter is what our faith is based on. Without this interaction between Abram and God, there would not be a conversation for us Christian's worth having. Let us dive into it.

God appears to Abram in a vision, and they have a conversation. God tells Abram that God is Abram's shield and his reward. Abram retorts with something along the lines of, that's great and all, but I don't have any children who will inherit that. Because of the barrenness in our life, all my stuff is going to go to Eliezer, one of my servants. God then establishes God's covenant with Abram, "Then the word of the LORD came to him: 'This man will not be your heir, but a son coming from your own body will be your heir.' He took him outside and said, 'Look up at the heavens and count the stars—if indeed you can count them.' Then he said to him, 'So shall your offspring be" (Gen 15:4&5, NIV).

We should all be pretty familiar with this covenant. But we tend to ignore what happened next. After Abram believes that this will come to pass, he also wants reassurance. After all, God first establishes that all people on earth will be blessed through Abram (Gen 12:3), so a little reassurance would always be nice (after all it's not like it's a major promise or anything), and because part of the covenant is the inheritance of land, God responds to Abram's asking for assurance in a way that those living in the ancient Near East would have understood at the time. God tells Abram to get a heifer, goat, ram (all of which must be three years old), a dove, and a young pigeon. Abram does this and note he doesn't ask what he needs to do with them. Abram already knows what needs to be done, so he proceeds to cut all but the birds in half and arrange them opposite of one another so that the blood would run down from where they are and create a kind of path.

In the ancient Near East, animals were slaughtered as a way to seal an oath, and a curse was accepted along the lines of, if I am to break this oath, may I become like this slaughtered animal.[1] Abram, being familiar with this type of oath fixes the animals as such and waits on God's orders for what to do next. Abram expects to go through this path with God and take up his side and responsibility of the oath, the blessed to be a blessing. As he waits, Abram becomes a bit tired as the sun sets, and he falls into a deep sleep, and a thick and dreadful darkness came over him (Gen 15:12) which makes sense given the weight of the situation. But what happens next? God appears to Abram and states that even though Abram's descendants will be slaves in a foreign land, they will return to this land God has promised, essentially saying this covenant will be fulfilled.

In the darkness, a smoking firepot with a blazing torch appear and they go down the blood line that was established. God is essentially saying, if this covenant I have made with you is not fulfilled, if I do not give you descendants, if they do not go into slavery, if I do not free them and bring them back to this land I have promised you, if all the people of earth are not blessed through the children of Abram, may I be like these animals and die. If God fails to fulfill God's part of the covenant, God will become like the animals. If Abram or Abram's line fails to fulfill the covenant, God will become like the animals. After all, God moved down the blood path without Abram, taking up all of the responsibility for what is to come.

This is followed by the birth of Ishmael and the covenant of circumcision, which is when Abram became Abraham. God again reestablishes God's covenant with Abraham of descendants and land, in that Sarai (now Sarah) will give birth to Isaac.

1. Weinfield, *Covenant of Grant*, pg. 185.

PORTION FOUR: VAYERA (GEN 18:1-22:24)

And finally, we make it to the last portion this book will cover. When we meet Abraham in Chapter 18, he is hanging out with God, chatting in the opening of his tent when Abraham sees three strangers riding by. When he sees this, he rushes over to them, essentially placing God on hold while he jumps at the opportunity to provide hospitality for these three messengers. Now, if you've heard the start of this story, there may be a chance you've heard that these three messengers represent the Trinity. Let us just throw that out right now: that is not the case and there is no evidence of that other than there are three people present. Most likely, given what we know in the text to this point, they are angels. So, keep that in mind: not the Trinity, but angels. After grabbing their attention, Abraham begs them to come rest at his tent and he will bring a "morsel"[2] of bread and they can go on their way. After they oblige and follow him back to his tent, Abraham goes to prepare for the feast. Finding Sarah, he has her prepare around 16 pounds (three seahs) of bread, while he goes to select the best and most tender calf for the meal. Along with some curds and milk, the food has been prepared and the messengers eat under the trees.

So, let's pause and look at how Abraham views hospitality. There are three strangers passing by and he decides to put God on hold while he runs out and seeks the opportunity to serve these people. Saying he wants to provide them only a bite of bread, he prepares an entire meal to ensure that there is enough for them should they need or want it. He goes out of his way to make sure that the stranger is cared for and is treated with the utmost respect and dignity. Keep this in mind—it will come up again (although not in the way you may expect).

After they are done eating, one of the messengers asks where Sarah is, and upon hearing she is in the tent, he tells Abraham that he will be back in a year and Sarah will have a son. Overhearing in disbelief, Sarah laughs and questions it because she will be 100 by that time. Responding, God spits back to Abraham, did

2. Lexicon-Concordance, line 6.

she really just scoff at what I had my guy say about her? Does she really believe this won't happen? Sarah, being nervous about it, says she didn't laugh, and God was like, yeah girl, you did. I love this interaction between them. I find it funny, especially because you have Sarah lying directly to God and God's not punishing or separating from her; God just gives her crap for it. After this, God contemplates whether or not God should hide what God is about to do from Abraham—committing the impending destruction of Sodom and Gomorrah.

God contemplates with God's self on whether or not to share this upcoming information with Abraham, because God knows full well how big the nation of Abraham will be but also, that Abraham will be more compassionate and just then God will be in this moment. Deciding not to hide this, God tells Abraham that things are so bad in Sodom and Gomorrah that the outcry has reached God, and because their sin is so great, God will go down and check out what is actually going on. So, the messengers head that way. After they leave, Abraham confronts God on what is about to happen. At this point, we still really have no idea why God chose Abraham out of everyone on earth. As I said at the beginning of Abraham's story, there are many schools of thought on this, and one is that Abraham was the most just person on earth, even more just than God is. We see this illustrated in the following passage. Abraham starts by asking God if God will sweep away the righteous with the wicked and goes on to say if there are at least 50 righteous people, God would surely not wipe away the wicked because of the righteous. In a stunning moment of passive aggressiveness, Abraham even goes so far to say in Gen 18:25 (NRSV), "Far be it from you to do such a thing to kill the righteous with the wicked, treating the righteous and the wicked alike. Far be it from you! Will not the Judge of the earth do what is just?"

This is Abraham taking a jab right at God and what happened with the flood. At a time when all the peoples of the earth were just terrible, there did not seem to be a standard on the righteous to wicked ratio for when to not destroy a place. One can argue that Abraham is challenging God as to whether or not God has changed and repented for God's previous actions. This is a huge moment, because Abraham is calling God to be better, to commit to the same standard that God is trying to hold Abraham to in being a blessing to all nations. And so, this back and forth continues until Abraham convinces God that if there are at least 10 righteous people in a city full of wickedness, God will not destroy it. Now two of the messengers (not three anymore, because one of them already delivered their message they were sent to give: the announcement of Isaac's birth in less than a year) arrive to the gates of Sodom in the evening. And so, begins Genesis 19.

Lot sits at the gateway, when we see this in the text, it could mean he acting as a gatekeeper of sorts. When we last left Lot, he was rescued and so as far as we know was still setting up his tent outside of Sodom, a place that was well watered like the garden of the LORD (this should evoke imagery of the garden of Eden). It was then we found out that Sodom was a pretty wicked and nasty place to be. Now we see Lot sitting at the gateway where things happened in cities, we see this time and again later on in the text and in extra biblical sources so we are to assume that Lot has been an active part of the city of Sodom for some time to earn this spot. So, upon seeing the angels, Lot bows and asks the angels to come to his house where they can wash their feet, stay the night, and then leave the next day. They refuse and state that they are going sleep in the town square but Lot's response is so insistent that they decided to end up staying in Lot's house. After they get to the house, Lot prepares, some food and bakes bread without yeast, and they went to go to bed. Eventually we are told, "all the men from every part of the city of Sodom—both young and old—surrounded the house. They called to Lot, 'Where are the men who came to you tonight? Bring them out to us so that we can have sex with them'" (Gen 19:4,5; NIV).

This passage has been used to justify the demonization of homosexuals, but that could not be further from what is happening right here. Unfortunately, this passage and much of the Bible has been hijacked by those who just want to control others and recreate humanity in their image while claiming it is God's. Up until this point, this entire passage has been about hospitality. All we know about Sodom at this point is that it is a city full of sin, that is on land that resembles Eden. Let's compare how the messengers were received by Abraham and Lot.

Abraham saw three men, ran up to them, begged them to come to his tent so they could have some water to cool off, and so that Abraham could provide a bite of bread and they could refresh themselves to be on their way. When they agree and go back to Abraham's tent, Abraham prepares a feast for them. Lot sees them, asks them to stay in his house so they could wash their feet, sleep, and leave the next day. After they refuse, Lot insists they stay and after agreeing he makes a meal with unleavened bread which says a lot about how long they are welcome in his house, because it takes less time to cook and eat unleavened bread than bread with yeast. So, what does hospitality have to with the people of Sodom and their sins? In a book called *Pirkei Avot*, found within the Talmud, something everyone should read, ancient Rabbis talk about various teachings on different passages of the Hebrew Bible. In it, we find something every Christian should know, "There are four types of people: One who says, 'What is mine is yours, and what is yours is mine' is a boor. One who says, 'What is mine is mine, and what is yours is yours—this is a median characteristic; others say this is the characteristic of Sodom. One who says, 'What is mine is yours, and what is yours is yours' is a pious person. And one who says, 'What is mine is mine, and what is yours is mine' is a wicked person."[3]

According to this rabbinical teaching, someone from Sodom believes what they have is theirs and theirs alone, and what the person that came to them had belonged to them alone. This is the type of action displayed by Lot's initial invitation to stay. This is the opposite of how Abraham acts. So, it shouldn't be surprising if this is the case, that all the men of town would come to shame them in an act of forced sexual violence and aggression, against the wills of the messengers because the men of Sodom do not want to share resources.

3. Maimonides, *Pirkei Avot,* 5:10.

Two more mouths showing up that, in their minds, probably don't belong there means resources will be used up that belong to Sodom. The concept of hospitality does not exist to the men of Sodom. Ezekiel 16:49 affirms this when the transgressions of Sodom are called out as being arrogant, overfed and under concerned, and they did not help the poor or the needy. They had no stomach for hospitality. This is the reason given by the narrator of Genesis for wiping them off the map. Because Lot showed hospitality to the messengers, he is given a warning of this impending destruction let us not forget the fact that Lot offered up his daughters to be on the receiving end of this sexual assault and violent aggression instead of the messengers. After Abraham argued with God and negotiated down to one righteous person being present in a city to save it from destruction, there is no righteous person present to stop the downfall of Sodom. A place reminiscent of Eden, a place that could have helped so many but instead decided to build walls to keep out those in need of help, turned to salt and sand. What was something as comparable to the garden of the LORD was now a baren space where it would be next to impossible to grow food. While evacuating from this end of the world image of the death and destruction of Sodom, Lot, and his daughter's escape.

In Genesis 22, we see the birth of Isaac. Finally, the fruit of the covenant has come from Sarah. This leads to the sending off of Ishmael and Hagar by Sarah's command, which God goes along with. Let us revisit a little thing I wrote about earlier, the Binding of Isaac. God starts up a conversation with Abraham by saying to take his only son Isaac and to offer him up as a burnt offering in the region of Morah at a place God will show Abraham. Abraham does not argue with God about this command. Now, I have sat under this passage in various times and places and in evangelical teachings, the one consistent thing I've found is they all tend to teach that Abraham has enough faith that his son will be spared, and this was a test all along.

I completely reject that teaching. Here is the guy that went toe to toe with God on the destruction of Sodom and the preservation of life, and the child he has waited for that will be the lineage for the covenant, is now demanded as a meal for God and Abraham goes along with it. So, Abraham has his only son, convinced that God will provide a lamb for the offering, and he and Isaac go up to the mountain for the sacrifice. After Abraham built the altar, he assaults Isaac, binds him up, and lays him on top of the wood to be sacrificed. Once Abraham reaches his hand up with the knife to kill Isaac, there is a dynamic shift in two relationships that will not recover.

The first, and most obvious shift is among Abraham and his family. Here is the son he had been waiting on, and the trust that was there is there no longer. After all, nothing has shown up to be sacrificed; from Isaac's perspective, God has really not provided. But also, this deep sense of severed trust from Abraham to Isaac is something that cannot be rebuilt. After they depart from here, we are told that they all leave the mountain and head to Beersheba, where Abraham stays, and his servants and Isaac move on. Abraham does not return home to Sarah while she is still alive. After all, how can you face someone who you've struggled through infertility with, only to try and offer your son as a burnt sacrifice?

Secondly, there is God and Abraham. Once the knife is raised to kill Isaac, Abraham no longer hears directly from God anymore; it is now a messenger that relays everything from God to him. Abraham stopped having this deep relationship with God, so there must have been a failure on Abraham's part to cause this rift. This unique call to Abraham from God to offer Isaac, the fruition of the covenant with God, and no word is brought up against this. This specific call to Abraham does not really apply to our own lives, yet we've been brought up to be on the verge of sacrificing everything at the whim, or test, of God instead of standing up to argue against, it like Abraham did with Sodom.

8

Bible Groundwork Wrap Up

THAT WAS A LOT of information, and there is no doubt some questions that will linger. What do I do with it? Does it matter? Why should I care about a working knowledge of the first few portions of Genesis? Well, I would argue the reason is, it deeply impacts your relationship with God, the divine, whatever you want to call it. Most of my life, I have not thought very highly of who I am, and what I have done. Breaking any rule, upsetting anyone no matter how little the transgression makes me feel awful. So, someone like me who assumed my entire life I was not good, when I was told by those in the church that I actually was not, and no matter what I do I cannot do anything good, it affects everything else.

This really influenced how I looked at God, and it made me not want to be a part of whatever God was doing. Why should I grovel at the feet of something that intentionally made me to fail? A common thing I said after I screwed something up was, well what do you expect? I'm a piece of crap. Until I realized total depravity does not help, thoughts like that were rooted and affirmed by this understanding of a God who separated God's self from humanity because of a mistake made once. A lot is revealed about the character of God in these passages. We see that God is compassionate in that God addresses the trauma of the garden scene, shame, God is remorseful and heartbroken over the state of creation, God present in the recreation, and God is hopeful in the future of humanity with Abraham.

We see God willing to take up the sword against God's self if Abraham's line does not fulfill the covenant (which will later happen with Jesus' resurrection), God is able to be put on hold while Abraham cares for strangers, God is righteously angry that justice is not shown to the foreigner in need, and God is taken to task over the destruction of creation or any city for that matter. God is faithful, as seen with the fulfillment of the covenant by the birth of Isaac, and God is tested with the binding of Isaac.

The emotions that are on display with the character of God are the emotions that we share every day. These emotions are divinely inspired. And the best part is, this is just one interpretation of these stories. This is a drop in a bucket of water during a rainstorm compared to what is out there especially if you read the Jewish perspective, and you really need to. Pulling the curtains back and looking at all these stories in a new light, especially the garden narrative, inform how we view God and how we decide to engage with God. From the beginning, they are not static but growing, like a garden. This whole thing, relationship, whatever, that we decide to opt into (or unfortunately is sometimes forced onto us by family or pressuring friends) is an ever—growing, ever—evolving thing that we are told not to test or challenge because of God's authority.

In the first few portions of this book that is paramount to our faith, we see all of these notions being challenged. It is good and right to question, push back, and figure out what the right thing is to do. After all. the ancient Israelites who wrote it included the gods of their oppressors, as discussed. Whether you ascribe to sola scriptura (scripture alone), sola fide by (faith alone), or sola gratia (by grace alone), this can help inform how you view the Being that wants you to be the best possible version of you—by being your authentic self and giving a crap about the justice due to the poor, foreign, widow, or orphan.

So now that we have seen this character of God (hopefully in new light), what do we do with it? Is there more to it? What does life look like with a God who does not think you are a piece of crap from the moment you are born?

9

The Names of God
and What They Say About Them

FOR ALMOST A CALENDAR year, my father and I split our time between Toledo and Dayton Ohio. My immediate family lived in Dayton but after my father's business went under, he found a job in Toledo where my mother's family from. I was just going into the first grade and the classes were all filled up, so I was to be sent forty—five minutes from my house (each way) to a school my parents did not want me to attend. With that in mind, they decided to enroll me in an elementary school in Toledo and I would go up there to live with my grandparents and father while my family tried to transition to Northwest Ohio. We would spend Monday through Friday afternoon in Toledo, and then drive down to Dayton for the weekend. Spend time with my siblings and mom. It was a very weird period in our lives. During this time, my dad was my best friend. And since then, even though we have very different views and opinions on a few things, we are still close.

This made it easy when I was growing up to accept, the predominate way I heard God described is not only male, but as a good father. However, that is not the case with everyone. I did not hold completely to the idea of an overly masculine God, I knew from reading just Genesis alone, that God has many attributes we flat out ignore because they do not fit that God as a good father image. As my reconstruction went on, I started reading the different names of God and getting past that binary understanding I grew up with. This not only deepened my understanding of who God can be at times, but it also helped me understand the acts of everyday divinity we bestow upon one another when we exhibit those characteristics. By everyday divinity, I mean the grace, acceptance, forgiveness, and love that we ought to be attempting in our interactions with one another.

Every time we name God as someone/something, we immediately alienate God from everything else God is. God is just one word we in the Abrahamic traditions (Judaism, Islam, and Christianity) use to describe the force from which all life has come and will hopefully return to. There are so many times a different name is used to describe what or who God is in the original Hebrew. American evangelicals have a hard time equating the idea that Jesus and God are on the same level, because we don't understand how to practice proper monotheism. In learning some of the names God possesses and their meanings, it may help us tear down some of those walls.

There are many names of God. This was not leaned on or taught too heavily in the evangelical culture I cut my teeth around because it can be confusing and causes people ask potentially uncomfortable questions. When going through the depths of reconstruction it is important to go through them to get a greater sense of the being or deity that people have worshiped for generations. It also helps us see into the greater depths of this God and be okay in the not knowing, or the empty spaces our faith can sometimes lead us to.

So, we are going to start by looking at a few commonly used names, then look at where this is going because we are experiencing a seismic shift in organized religion right now. We just spent time looking at the ever—evolving character of God from the beginning of humanity's interactions with God, let us look at the names. After all, a lot can be known or assumed by the names you give something or someone. We are going to focus on what they mean, and why they are an important foundation to build on.

Although there are a few names used for God in Genesis, the name El Shaddai or Shaddai is given by Abraham when God appears and announces God's self right before the covenant of circumcision. This name typically is translated to God Almighty and it is usually used in a masculine way. Now, to be clear, this may be the most controversial of the names and interpretations we go over in this chapter, and I know I may not be right in this, but the conclusion I come to is the one I have been most familiar with. When the Septuagint was being translated from the Hebrew to Greek, it may have been thought the name came from the word meaning to either overpower or destroy, shadad. It is also used when God tells Jacob in Genesis 35 to be fruitful and multiply throughout the earth, then again in when Jacob gives out blessings before his (spoiler alert) death. We find when God reaches Jacob he says, "…because of your father's God, who helps you, because of the Almighty, who blesses you with blessings of the sky above, blessings of the deepest springs below, blessings of the breast and womb" (Gen 49:25, NIV).

Because Shaddai is used again in this passage for the name of God, and because the passage is connected with the blessings of the womb and breast (the root word of breast is shadayim) the two are connected. This connection has caused quite a large number of people over the generations to think that the actual root word of El Shaddai is not shadad but shadayim. That El Shaddai, the name connected with fertility blessings in Genesis is actually a more fertile and feminine side of God, the "God of breasts"[1], God is a God of nourishment and fertility instead of overpowering and destruction. So often we hear about the destructive and punitive God of the Old Testament, but that doesn't seem to fit in with this name.

The second name was given when El Shaddai was no longer enough, and that is the name YHWH (Yahweh). This is the most frequently used of the names, and the letters that make up the name is also called the tetragrammaton. The tetragrammaton is

1. Baile, *God of Breasts*, pg. 240–256.

the personal name of God, and it is so highly respected by some in the Jewish faith, they do not even utter the name and instead use a different word, like Adonai. And a lot of times when written out, the vowels will be removed as a sign or form of respect for the name. I practice this vowel removal in my personal life to remind myself there is something set apart with the divine that is bigger and vaster than myself. This is the name God gave to Moses in the form of the Burning Bush, then again on the mountain top in the infamous, I AM WHO I AM moment in Exodus 3.

In Hebrew, the tetragrammaton is also in the third person, which causes something interesting to happen to the name and the way it is interpreted. It means "to be"[2] and this has caused a lot of people over many generations to think the original name to mean, "He who brings into being."[3] However, because of this third person name, when God has the moment with Moses on the mountain top the name means, "He who is self—existing, self—sufficient,"[4] and also "He who lives."[5] Since this is the personal name of God in Hebrew and throughout the Bible, the idea of life has been connected with God on a very intimate level.[6]

A third name of this divine being is Elohim. While YHWH is singular and also in the third person, this name of God is plural. It conveys the majesty and excellence of God, while at the same time respecting the awesomeness and great dignity of God. What is fascinating about this is the root meaning of Elohim is unknown. The closest anyone can guess is that it may have come from a verb in Arabic (alih), and Elohim translates into either, "He who is the object of fear or reverence"[7] or "He with whom one who is afraid takes refuge."[8]

2. My Jewish Learning, *The Tetragrammaton,* line 15
3. My Jewish Learning, *The Tetragrammaton,* line 17.
4. Jewish Encyclopedia, *Names of God,* line 55.
5. Jewish Encyclopedia, *Names of God,* line 56.
6. Jewish Encyclopedia, *Names of God,* line 57.
7. Jewish Encyclopedia, *Names of God,* line 106.
8. Jewish Encyclopedia, *Names of God,* line 107.

A quick note on fear of God: I once heard it described by my friend Mitch as standing on the edge of the Grand Canyon, or as I have experienced it, being on the open ocean. The vast and overwhelming awesomeness which surrounds you could swallow you up in a second or bring destruction, which is somehow calming. This idea of a larger thing than you, that is awe—inspiring, beautiful, and naturally terrifying at the same time. When I talk about the fear of God, this is what I am referring to. Not the terrible, list—checking, waiting for you to screw up monstrosity the oppressive gate—keeping patriarchy has dreamed up.

When I was a kid going to the occasional Sunday school class, I heard quite often that God is jealous. That name is El Kanno (Qanna). The first time it shows up is in Exodus 20:5. The passage talks about how the Israelites must not bow down to another god, and that God will punish the children of those who do to the third and fourth generation, but for those who love God and keep God's commandments, God will show love to the generations. This is a hard passage and should be wrestled with and acknowledged, because this is a small part of the character of God that gets too much credit and attention. However, what is not talked about is how this jealous demeanor is less about envy like coveting someone's property or envy over a job. It is jealous as it applies to marriage.[9] Marriage language is used quite often to describe the relationship between God and the Israelites. We see this a lot in Paul's writings about Christians, Jesus, and the church. After all, Jesus refers to himself as a bridegroom (Mark 2:18–20), so this should not be surprising. But because of that, it needs to be placed in its proper context. The jealousy of a mad lover after they have caught their spouse having an affair, (Golden Calf at the base of the mountain, anyone?) makes sense. This is another intimate aspect into the character of God.

A name given to God by Hagar, after she fled because of Sarah's mistreatment in Genesis 16, is "El Roi."[10] This naming is brought about after an angel of God announces to Hagar that she

9. Poblete, *The Names of God*, lines 1–14.

10. Hebrew 4 Christians, line 81.

is pregnant and tells her to return to her slave master. "You are the One who sees me," Hagar says (Gen 16:13, NIV). This to me is powerful. In the midst of the abuse she has received, she is given a child and is recognized by the God of Abraham, El Shaddai, who has provided so far for them. This also feels like a first hint at God watching over and out for the oppressed. And it does not go unnoticed by Hagar.

One last name that should be mentioned before we move on is the name Abba. This is not only the name of one of the greatest bands to ever grace Eurovision, but it literally means "father"[11] It can be said that Abba conveys an intimacy between the creation and creator. It is also found in the New Testament.

So, to perform a brief recap:

1. El Shaddai, thought to be overpowering and destructive but may actually mean nurturing, fruitful, and feminine.

2. YHWH, the personal name that is revered, and self—sustaining, and the one who will bring all things into being.

3. Elohim, the attribute which causes wonder and fear, but also someone to whom one can run and be safe with.

4. El Kanno, a jealous lover.

5. El Roi, the God who sees.

6. Abba, dearest father.

Looking at this list, one thing is for sure: there are a lot of male, or masculine attributes to the names of God, which is too bad, considering as we know it, God has no gender. In my experience with the evangelical church, we have latched on to this idea of God being the good, Zeus—looking father figure, basically projecting what every straight white male pastor has ever wanted to be but falls short of. When this become the predominate image of God, the name "God" shifts away from being an all—encompassing word that includes the God who sees, the jealous lover, the nurturing mother, the one to be safe with, and the self—sustainer.

11. Dictionary Online, line 2.

The view of God becomes broken. There is a reason why trying to nail down all the attributes of God is like nailing gelatin to a wall. God is so much bigger than what we know God to be. In order to move toward being open to that, we need a foundation of who we know God can be—something void of this Zeus imagery or this fatherly Santa Claus that treats prayer like a naughty or nice list. Can you imagine a world where we leaned harder into the nurturing, motherly side of the creator? Imagine a world where we do not tell people they need to give everything up to a God who will be there like a good parent, when they have only experienced abuse and degradation from their parents.

I wanted to assemble some of these names because if we look at them closely, they touch on different attributes and characteristics of the divine being who brought all into existence. This Being is not a "one name fits all" situation. In fact, when churches (individually or globally) try and do that, they have created an idol they are worshiping that sliver of God, instead of opening themselves up to the vast, unknown, rich pool that is God. And right now, the American evangelical church is in a place where a lot of people are starting to move past that language, they are naming new attributes, and disregarding the baggage of this former sacred language. In looking at this new language, I highly recommend the book, *Learning to Speak God from Scratch* by Jonathan Merritt. More fundamental churches are doubling down on their views of God because for some people, it is a scary time. We are treading through previously unknown waters, but it is an exciting time. We are all on the forefront of this new leaning into God and being okay with being open to what comes next, which is why we must address who we have known God to be.

10

Jesus: Human Trolly Problem, Wrong Place at the Wrong Time, or Someone Completely Different?

WHEN I WAS A child, my parents took me to Sunday school to a Baptist Church in Toledo, Ohio. The first Sunday I was there; I was introduced to Jesus. Sitting there in my sweet blazer, red tie, white shirt, and khaki pants I watched as my teachers set up a projector and started to tell me a story. It wasn't about a child born in a manger. It wasn't about a Jewish man walking around the countryside healing the sick. It wasn't about teaching the masses. It was about a man who brought his son to work that day. The man worked in a train yard surrounded by bridges and his job was to switch the tracks so that trains could safely cross the water. This particular day, instead of hanging out in the tower with the father like he usually did, the son decided to climb down and explore the world below. While he did so, the father continued his work and noticed the 10 am train with fifty passengers coming right on schedule. In fact, one could say it was coming as planned. It was then the father heard his son crying, and peering down to see what was going on, saw his son was trapped in the gears of the mechanism that changes the tracks for that same train.

The father radioed the train's conductor and told him what was going on, and he was informed that if they were to apply the brakes, they would still go off the track and everyone onboard would die, because there wasn't enough time. The father had a choice: He could go down and rescue his son, oh, and I forgot to mention, this is his only child, and everyone on board the train would die. Or he could move the gears and sacrifice his son to save the fifty people. While thinking about it, he decided it was better for his son to die and save the fifty people.

I was then informed that the son was Jesus, the operator was God, and that is what Jesus did for all of us. If we didn't accept Jesus into our hearts as our personal Lord and Savior, we would burn in hell forever. I was told it would be like burning our finger on a toaster but over our whole body forever and ever amen. Having burnt my finger on a toaster that morning, I stayed after class, said a prayer, and was saved. It wasn't until I sat in my first semester philosophy class that I learned I had known the trolly problem since I was a child.

This was a really screwed up way to learn about Jesus, but honestly, I cannot imagine a more American evangelical way of learning about him. We treat him like a guy whose only purpose was to die so that God could forgive sins. At least, that is what I was taught and at one point taught and believed myself. Why do we teach this? Is this all there is to the humanity of Jesus? Born so that I could say a prayer, be a complete jerk my entire life, poop all over the oppressed, deny human rights to others, then die and end up in some form of paradise? Well, let's get into the guts of this idea and see where we come out.

So, who was Jesus? The easy answer is, he was a Jewish man, born around the turn of the first century in a Middle Eastern country known as Israel. This means he was most likely not caucasian but of olive/brownish complexion. He gained popularity within areas of his community, where he was ultimately sentenced to be crucified by the state and died. In an Arabic translated manuscript from the tenth century by the Jewish historian Josephus, *Testimonium Flavianum,* had this to say about him, "At this time there was a wise man who was called Jesus. And his conduct was good, and [he] was known to be virtuous. And many people from among the Jews and the other nations became his disciples. Pilate condemned him to be crucified and to die. And those who had become his disciples did not abandon his discipleship. They reported that he had appeared to him three days after his crucifixion and that he was alive; accordingly, he was perhaps the Messiah concerning whom the prophets have recounted wonders."[1]

According to singer/songwriter Woody Guthrie, he was a hardworking carpenter that traveled through the land. He was followed by crowds of working people that would sing and shout very gaily. And Jesus told the preachers and bankers to sell their jewelry and give their money to the poor. With the help of Judas and the backlash of this radical pronouncement, the cops and soldiers nailed him to a cross. Because of this Jesus died and was put into the grave.[2]

Our ideas about Jesus are filled out a little bit more when we use religious texts depending on which Gospel, because all four contain different accounts. Jesus then becomes someone who was born towards the beginning of the first century in a town called Bethlehem, which was in the nation state of Israel under Roman occupation. Afterward, a king tried to put him to death because three grown men who were looking for him made the mistake of visiting the king first. After he became a refugee in Egypt, these men met up with this child. It should be pointed out here that the travelers did not seek to become converted. They, and the Gospel's author were content with the three worshiping and acknowledging the status of Jesus and then leaving. They laid gifts at his feet, then took a different route home and ignored the command of a king.

Then Jesus is older, entering his ministry and going around the countryside teaching in parables, feeding those in need, healing the sick, and raising people from the dead. At some point, his

1. Pines, *Arabic Testimonium Flavianum,* pg. 16.
2. Guthrie, *Jesus Christ,* lines 3–30.

disciple, Judas, became overzealous and wanted to show everyone Jesus was Messiah, to the point that he made a deal that ends up going very badly. This results in the death of Jesus by crucifixion, three days pass, and he rises from the dead only to be unnoticed initially as a gardener to the women trying to pay their respects. Jesus then hangs out with his disciples, and finally ascends to heaven. So, what is the point of all of this?

In October of 2011 I interrupted a local pastor who was studying the text at a coffee shop. We had met once before, and I thought I would ask his perspective on a passage I was prepping for Bible study. The aforementioned Don wanted to back up, so he asked me, why did Jesus die on the cross? This question sent me into a tailspin of uncertainty when the usual Sunday school answers did not cut it. And he just kept asking me that same question until I ran out of answers. I referred to Jesus as a human sacrifice and heard the retort of God abhorring human sacrifices (Deut. 18:10; Lev 18:21), Then I went for the tried and true John 3:16 answer of God giving up the one true offspring God had, his response was, for what? I tried to say it was for the forgiveness of our sins and the rest of humankind, and it was pointed out to me that God forgave sins before Jesus was a spark in Mary's eye. So, I was left struggling with how this supposed son of God fit into my faith in my traditional ways. Who cares if he was resurrected after three days if I could not figure out why he was here in the first place? This was when Don told me about Abraham and the covenant he had with God and explained it in a way I had never heard, and will share with you.

While I did a brief flyover of the text already in chapter seven, let us go into a deeper dive of Genesis 15: the blood oath, the fire, and the smoking pot. In this reading, God was sealing God's covenant with Abraham so that all peoples on earth would be blessed through his lineage and obtain the future promised land for the inhabitants. And to seal this, Abraham had to get specific animals, slaughter them, and line them up opposite of one another so that the blood flowed down and created a type of path. Instead of Abraham walking down it with God, God's self went down the path, symbolizing that if the covenant wasn't fulfilled, God would have to die. In the covenant God made with Abram, animals lined up and a blood path was created. When God passed through the path Abram was supposed to walk down with God, but he fell asleep, so God did it alone. When this happened, God took responsibility for the descendants of Abram and what happens if the covenant was no longer fulfilled. In the ancient Near East, if you preformed that oath but it was no longer fulfilled, you were able to kill the person for not upholding it. So, when Abram's descendants were no longer a blessing for all peoples, in theory, God could have held Abram accountable. But since God fulfilled the oath God's self, God is the one who has to pay the price for it. So, when I am asked about why Jesus had to die on the cross, where the Biblical support is for this, I point to Genesis 15.

While that is a great explanation of the crucifixion, the question remains, was it necessary? I don't think so. I think God could have let business as usual go on and let what happens happen. After all, Israel has never stopped being God's chosen people; with Jesus, the net was just cast wider over time to allow more people to participate in the covenant with Abraham. Paul never stopped being Jewish after his Damascus moment; he spent the rest of his life trying to figure out how to be more inclusive to those who were not born into the tribes.

So, who was Jesus? One answer is that Jesus was a man who spent his short time on earth refocusing the conversation around the Torah (not the oral law) to bend towards the justice—oriented code it was always meant to be. Having these conversations in person at this point in the conversation, someone usually stops me and brings up the "the poor will always be with us line" that Jesus casually threw out to his disciples. This line, in my experience, has justified a lot of evangelicals to not give money to those who ask, or just in general to not give a crap about the poor and marginalized. This cutting throwaway line is a call back to Deuteronomy 15 which opens with the command to cancel debts every seven years, a practice which is called Jubilee. If ancient Israel would have gone through with the Jubilee, following the Torah, and cancelled debts when they were supposed to, there may still have been some poor, and therefore, they were instructed to be open handed to those in need. It is a beautiful moment for me, to see Jesus cutting down those who think they know how things are because they think they uphold the teachings, only to be clapped back to this reexamination.

Something that should be pointed out when we consider the character of Jesus is that, although we have four different accounts of his life, the one thing that is consistent is that he always bends towards helping out the poor and oppressed. Jesus was, and is, a social justice activist and preacher because that is what this covenant called for. If we are to believe what we were taught about Jesus being the fulfillment of the law, that means he embodied the Torah. He lived how God would live if God were human. Which means, if you were to boil the Torah down to one question, it would be, what is the most life giving? Then that is what he represented. The constant outward actions of love, loving the lord our God, and love our neighbor as ourselves.

Here was a dude who was brought up on charges against the state, and instead of raising a finger against them and causing an uprising, he went in peace. He lived the line that he taught and died. At his death, the curtain ripped in the holy of holies within the Temple. The rending of this garment is often overlooked because we as Christians ignore not only imagery in the Bible but biblical literacy itself. When Joseph "died" and Jacob was shown the "proof", he tore his garment, and the same happened with King David when he heard about the passing of King Saul. The ripping of the curtain represents the mourning of God, a parent weeping for their child. We honestly do not know how to deal with the humanity of Jesus, because we have never had to. We have always focused on his divinity. And that is okay. It is not wrong to be back and forth on how to feel about that. One thing that is important to recognize is that his presence allowed a whole new people group to be able to bless others through their actions, even though many of us have fallen short of that. This guy has shown how we should live: caring for the poor not just in word but deed, living our convictions, and being in relationship with the divine, however that looks. The life of Jesus is such a compelling idea to emulate, we should be working towards living that way instead of just shouting about it from social media mountaintops.

What Jesus taught his disciples according to the accounts we have, is that something more is expected of those who decide to live a life within Christianity. What does a life like that look like? It includes things like engaging in conversations about God and questioning bad theology in order for everyone involved in the conversation to stop gatekeeping and to let others take a seat at the table, and to grow. John the Baptist announced the kin-dom of heaven was at hand, Jesus invites us into it, by participating every day in taking care of our neighbor, foreigner, widow, orphan, the poor, and ushering in the age to come. After all, who cares if he was raised from the dead if there will always be the poor that are in need without anyone to help? Do we not deny the cross by ignoring those we have harmed actively and passively? I think about the sheep and the goats in Matthew 25 quite often, and how I used to be so concerned I would end up in the goat category. Claiming to be the followers of Jesus but not having done any of the physical work along the way. To be clear I am not trying to open a works versus grace argument, that's for much more educated people to discuss. But the action of ignoring the plight of the least of these, Jesus seems to take seriously to the point of some eternal separation. Jesus, allegedly knowing of his impending death, decides that this is going to be one of his last living teachings.

What concerned me so much with this parable in my youth, aside from the clear danger of a fiery punishment, was that everyone seemed to be so confused about who was in and who was out. Everyone in that parable is surprised, the sheep because they just saw a need and went to help, and the goats because they thought they were following Jesus but missed a big part of the follow. Maybe they were taught that way? But shouldn't the punishment fall on the teachers? Were the goats the teachers?! All that to say, there are so many teachings and parables found in the gospels that can be used for awful things. This one alone can cause people to live in fear that they are not doing enough. But what does enough mean? Jesus does not put a number on how many people were clothed, fed, visited, or cared for. An argument can be made that doing it once was enough. That is why this parable brings me so much hope now, we put the limits and barriers on what it means to be enough when following the teachings of Jesus. What do numbers matter when the humanity is completely forgotten about?

If you get to a point when you are no longer welcome in the church you grew up in for asking questions to try and make sense of your faith, and you are trying to figure out what to keep, just remember: after Jesus taught at his home synagogue, the people walked him over to the cliff the town was built on to try and throw him off it. If there is anyone who understands what growth is like, and no longer being welcome because of change in theology, lifestyle, or whatever, Jesus understands. One more thing: this is the same guy who believes in his followers as much as they believe in him, and to paraphrase John 14, he encourages us that we will do far greater things than he did.

11

Reconstructing God and Jesus

THE CHURCH SEEMS TO be on that cycle of reinventing itself in some way every 500 years. This is not a new concept and Phyllis Tickle wrote about it in her book, *The Great Emergence: How Christianity is Changing and Why*. There is a schism or break which propels things forward at great personal loss to the people trying to reform. Some of the things I write in this book may cost me the ability to get a job at some churches further down the line, but that is nothing compared to the people who have been forced out of their local churches because their executions of belief challenge the status quo. How do we make the church more inclusive, where all are actually welcomed to explore, push back, and go forward arm in arm, into the great unknown? We name what is going on. We need a new church, for a new generation—not one that is a copy and paste of the old guard.

Over the next couple of chapters, I will re—touch upon almost everything I've covered so far in the book. The goal of this is to give some jumping off points towards rebuilding a faith that may not reflect what you grown up with but will leave you demanding more. Some parts may stay the same, or maybe a lot of it will change, and that's okay! It is very important to note that the experience and work of deconstruction and reconstruction is an ongoing process. You will probably never arrive to a perfect faith or practice, so do not be so hard on yourself or others if you find yourself frustrated in that spot. This is a long and arduous process, and it will look different for everyone.

So, the question must be asked: if I won't "arrive" to a place where I think I get "it", or where "it" works perfectly for me, then what is the point? Why all the work if I'm going to be at this continual tearing down and rebuilding? The process is worth it because you are worth it. Knowing who you are and what you believe and adjusting that as you continue to grow and learn, is worth it for you. The concrete answers were the ones that probably drove to deconstruction in the first place.

Often in life we build things and people up to what we want them to be, not what and who they actually are. We have done this same thing with God, and it sets up a false narrative. Broadly speaking, when most of us think of God, it is this grandpa—like figure who heavily resembles the ancient Greek god Zeus. There is a reason for this: Christianity historically absorbs other religions and takes on aspects of them to make things more palpable for those we are forcing to turn or burn. Because of this, all of our ideas of who God is started to form rigid outlines, especially when enforced from the pulpit. When these images start to crack and we sit in our first semester philosophy class, our faith starts to crumble and fall when the teacher quotes Nietzsche, "God is dead. God remains dead. And we have killed him. How shall we comfort ourselves, the murderers of all murderers? What was holiest and mightiest of all that the world has yet owned has bled to death under our knives: who will wipe this blood off us? What water is there for us to clean ourselves? What festivals of atonement, what sacred games shall we have to invent? Is not the greatness of this deed too great for us?"[1]

Evangelicals take the God is dead idea to an extreme it is not meant to go, especially when we are talking theatrically, but I digress. The idea behind it, at least the one I remember being taught is, what is left after your idea of God is dead? This question

---

1. Nietzsche, *Parable of the Madman*, lines 9–12.

is something a lot of post—evangelicals, or exvangelicals are not afraid to ask. This is deconstruction. Who is this dead god that fit your context and culture, that you left behind in order to find and search for God, or the divine? When we start this journey forward, we must examine if there are the things about the god, we are leaving behind that we would die without. Was there some good about the place we are leaving, and is it important to honor that and take what works with us? Now that the old white man god is dead, what is there about the divine that is different, and we get to explore?

First of all, as presented in this book, I work from the idea that God has no gender. The only time gender has been attributed to God or the divine in this book is when it has been quoted from an outside source. This is important for the inclusivity of God. This inclusivity makes God more attainable, more tangible, and more touchable. We are very used to the idea of God being the good father or represented with male pronouns. Those are attributes. To say that God acts in masculine and feminine ways at times is true. However, to say that God is strictly male, or female would not be true.

Chapter 9 explored some of the names of God. This idea was to show off that each name conveys a different attribute of who this divine source is, whether it is the personal name of YHWH, the self-sustaining God, or El Shaddai, the more nurturing, effeminate side. But the name "God" itself is, for some people, loaded with a lot of emotional or spiritual trauma. What do you call this semi-familiar thing with boundless attributes and characteristics? This thing that is always the same, while simultaneously changing over time (remember the Genesis account and how we saw that God matured and changed?) and has complex emotions, but also has no gender or pronoun to speak of? For my part, I still use the name God (if that hasn't been obvious enough throughout the book), but it has taken on a new and different meaning. Earlier I brought up Jonathan Merritt's book *Learning to Speak God from Scratch*, one area he explores the idea of saving and refurbishing sacred words in order to reclaim and renew them to strip them of their previous harm. I tend to fall in this camp because I believe there is still good in it, and I personally have not found many words that strike the right chord and convey the emotions I have been accustomed to. Merritt goes into greater detail on this, and the people who have transitioned from sacred language and I cannot recommend this book enough if this is something you are struggling with.

Let's set language aside and figure out who this center of religion is. We know from the story that God is either the creator or designer of all things and at one point sent a part of itself (Spirit) to dwell among humans. After all, this thing created wonderful sights like nebulas and Paul Rudd. People have been trying to connect with this spiritual fabric of reality since the beginning of time; it is what almost every major world religion is about, and we have appropriated practices in a way to stretch our Western minds to connect in this way. One of the most popular appropriated practices is yoga, and then there are the ones that do "Christian" yoga, which is a change in language and sometimes different names of the positions.

Most conservative Christians can agree that the Bible is absolute truth because it came from God, yet they cannot wrap their heads around the idea of God's absolute truth being sprinkled and sewn into different faiths, just because Jesus said he is the way, truth, light, and no one gets to the Father except through him. But if all truth comes from and is God, then by extension, any truth found anywhere is of God or the divine fabric of the universe. There is a tradition that talks about Moses standing at Mount Sinai getting ready to go up to the mountain, and God is speaking, and it is like thunder, which this tradition latches on to and said it was God speaking in all languages at once. God spoke to everyone in all languages at the same time so that all the world could hear God, whether or not they were listening. This is followed up during Pentecost, when we see the Spirit descend and fall on the apostles who start speaking in languages they previously did not know. So, this truth is spilling out to all of creation.

When I sat down to start rebuilding what I thought and believed about this universal being, that was a pretty good place to start. Now, there are a lot of sticky wickets in the Hebrew Bible about how God acts, which can be seen as condoning violence. It is important to wrestle with this and acknowledge its presence. But it is also important when dealing with those passages to ask whether or not the people God was instructing argued back like Abraham did. The reverence that has been drilled into our heads that we ought to have for God has gotten in the way of a tangible relationship where we have the ability to consent and could say no to whatever is instructed or planned.

Speaking of planning, let's talk about the "perfect plan" God has for our lives and the idea that God knows everything. I am not in the camp that believes everything happens for a reason, in order to slurp down the fact that life sometimes just sucks. There are multiple times in the Bible that God seems to forget about people or groups. I once worked in a church where the lead pastor taught from the pulpit that total control is total love. This is a picture of abuse, and I reject this view of God with every fiber of my being. Love is when you think someone may hurt themselves or make a mistake but be with them through that because they are free and of their own will. If we believe we have free will, then this must be part of that equation.

When it comes to violence in the Bible, one thing we have to ask ourselves is how is it reflected in the human Jesus. While David was apparently a man after God's own heart, which is horrible phrasing and emboldens bad people to do unspeakable acts and then fall back on that idea, Jesus is supposed to be God incarnate. How does Jesus handle violence? By saying turn the other cheek, which causes the violent one to treat you as an equal. But he does so much more too! Remember when Jesus tells people to cut their eye out instead of lusting after someone, which essentially translates to no matter what someone is wearing, it is on you to stop your feelings before you dehumanize someone? Because I am human, I want some humanity to interact with, whether it is historical Jesus or Biblical Jesus. When I was trying to re—figure out what I thought about him, I was always leaning into his humanity. He wept before Lazarus was raised from the dead showing that grief and vulnerability are natural and good parts of life. With Jesus, what we get is this physical manifestation of Torah. Taking care of the poor, ensuring that the powers that be understand where they are falling short, being okay with people showing up for what they need (healing, food, etc.) while not outwardly accepting him as messiah and then continuing on with his day.

How we respond to who God or Jesus is a really vital part to our humanity. I don't mean the morality part, because you can be a moral and good person outside of the known avenues of Christianity. Whether or not we ascribe to that worldview (which most of us do since we were born in the West) we all want someone to emulate, someone to affirm that our lives are on the right track. Who better than someone who wants to make sure the poor are taken care of, that the sick are healed, that those who have been in the back are now being taken care of first, and that those who betray us are forgiven in the end to emulate?

12

A New Church for a New Generation

BEFORE MY WIFE AND I moved to Columbus, we lived in Grand Rapids, Michigan. While living there, we had been members of a fairly well—known megachurch. We continued attending after the elders found a new lead pastor, but the teachings and teacher did not reflect what we had come to associate and love about the church. The Jewish roots that we had come to associate with it where being left behind in favor of a more liturgical approach, which is not necessarily a bad thing. I had personally felt like it was a step backward.

This was our local church. This was the church that I would listen to every Sunday via podcasts because I couldn't find one that better reflected my love of the Jewish roots. This was the place I could initially go to during my hurt from my pasts and just disappear into the people and try to hold on to what I believed. This was the place that I had experienced God and felt my call back into ministry after a few years of dark wandering when I thought I had waisted my life and time in it. The church I had loved, the one that had played a huge part in my growth for over a decade, had changed in a way where I no longer felt at home. And that is okay. The scales had been removed from my eyes, and whether or not it had always been that way, I realized it was (or had become) just another church where they say that all are welcome. However, the reality was that they, like many mainline evangelical churches, paid lip service while not being willing to take a stand with LGBTQIA+ brothers, sisters, and non—binary who have to justify their lives because we had the privilege to stay silent in a time where that is no longer an option.

During this time, my wife was in the throes of a master's degree, and we started talking a little about what a church plant would look like. Church planting was something that had always been in the background of the conversation while I was still in ministry, so it seemed like a good time to revisit it. I had this calling back into ministry I was trying to work out. Don and I had talked about branching off his church, and that seemed like a good option. After all, no one was busting down my door to hire me in that capacity, and we had a great group of people that would probably join us in that journey. So, the question rapidly became, what would this look like? But before we had the chance to lay the groundwork for this community, we had to move out of state for my wife's work. Classic. This question, however, has not left me and in fact seems to burn brighter and deeper. The church has endured thousands of years for a reason. There is something in it that intrinsically connects with people (not just through fear of death at the foot of the Christian oppressors), so there is something about it that should endure. But what will that look like in this time? What do we strip away and keep in this church rummage sale?

The tricky part about reforming any aspect of the Protestant church is that it is like herding cats. While the Catholic church has the Pope to be the final word on everything in that world, we have the paper pope (also known as the Bible) and any person, myself included, can pick it up and make some decree, however miss-educated and out of context. The church should be a place that has calloused hands, dirty fingernails, very diverse skin color, and sexual orientation. We (the church) claim to be God's representatives on earth and to follow in the footsteps of a Middle Eastern carpenter, but all we put forward are tan, blonde, or brown-haired Caucasians with bleached teeth and very little body fat (maybe dad bod is acceptable if we are lucky) and claim we are trying to lead people to Jesus and the life they live reflects that. The church works from a skewed premise in that typically, Jesus is treated as a personal savior for everyone. This is not big enough for the church, and it is embarrassing. The religious landscape of ancient Judaism was a communal one, but this has gotten lost in the history of Christianity. We were always meant to worship, live, and experience life together and this has vital repercussions to our individualized idea of faith. So how do we move forward? What do we do with a Jesus that is not meant to be my personal genie?

Well, that is part of the issue. Historically speaking, the church is not very good at change of any type, and the people that offered the opportunity to do that were killed as heretics or excommunicated. Adding an electric guitar or drum set to sanctuary worship caused some people to leave their churches. I get it, change is hard, especially when it comes to something that is taken so personally. The changes in the landscape must be reflected in the church. In an age where we are beautifully enriched by science, we need to drop the literal seven—day creation narrative. We know mental health is not caused by demons, and cancer isn't ghost in your blood that can be prayed out. We need to be better about exposing the people preying on those individuals and the abuse that comes from that. It is not rocket science. There are religious sects within the frameworks of Christianity that nurture and conceal abuse of various types, and that does not come from God or what we are supposed to stand for. So, in order to overhaul the church environment, it is critical to ask ourselves what is holding ourselves back? What I primarily mean by this is, are we as comfortable offering a seat to everyone the same way Jesus was? Most, at a glance will say yes, but let's dive a little bit deeper, because Jesus tended to cast a wider net than others.

Before we go any further, a note about the Pharisees and Sadducees. It is agreed upon by many that the modern rabbinic tradition within Judaism was born out of the tradition of the Pharisees.[1] Pharisees remained ritually clean at almost all times

1. Burns, *Pharisees and Rabbinic Judaism*, lines 25–29.

WE DON'T TRUST YOUR THEOLOGY

in the event they needed to perform the rites at the Temple at any time. They were so reverent for the commands of God they created the oral tradition and kept it like a fence around Torah so that they would not break a law of God even by mistake. Jesus' teachings were very much aligned with Hillel the Elder, who had established a school of thought that teachers were brought up in, and he was a Pharisee. It is, therefore, often thought by some that Jesus himself was a Pharisee. Why does this matter? Constantly throughout the text people find excuses to poop all over the Pharisees, in some cases going so far as to call someone a Pharisee if they do not agree with their viewpoint of Christianity. This is at best, anti—Jewish, and if this has been you in the past, it needs to stop. The Pharisees were not bad people. Neither were the Sadducees, so when we hear people doing this, we need to collectively cut it out.

Jesus arguing with them back and forth isn't the same type of argument we think of today. You could have disagreements on the interpretation of the text and still be great friends. A tradition from Shammai the Elder that emerged the same time as Hillel was around not agreeing with one another, yet remaining friends, "Although the two Houses were greatly at variance in their thinking, they were not rivals in the literal sense. As the Talmud states: 'They showed love and friendship towards one another.' In general, these controversies were regarded as the ultimate model of 'an argument for the sake of Heaven' — that is, disagreement without personal benefit."[2]

This approach to disagreement and conversations over the Bible is incredibly important and very freeing. When our salvation no longer relies on having the correct theology, but in one another engaging in community where all are welcome, it is a paradigm shift for the ages. And one that helps us move forward a bit. When, or if we land at a spot to freely ask these questions, we must take a step back and ask ourselves if we do not know for sure if Jesus really rose from the dead, or if there is this divine vastness that is embedded in all of creation, and last but not least, whether or not there is a spirit that nudges us on what to do. We are freed up to

2. Steinsaltz, *Talmudic Images*, pg. 10.

engage in conversations that used to be very hard. I am not trying to discount any interactions people have had with the spiritual realm, but what I am trying to say is we need to lean into our uncertainty and be honest about it. By starting there and answering honestly when Jim on a Sunday morning asks, "How's your heart?", you can be honest and tell him that this week you are not sure God exists and not be afraid that he will respond by saying you are wrong. Sure, there will always be people who go that route but your honesty being reflected back on a doubt or feeling he may not be willing to admit exists isn't your fault.

For a very long time, too much power has been held by the pulpit, and the Sunday morning experience has just morphed into a setting where people are happy with a McJesus and free soft drink. It has been used for generations in unhealthy ways and even though some churches understand how to keep it from becoming stale or corrupt, the issue stands that it acts as the voice of the community and not all members of the community are represented by it. In some communities it fails to show the diversity of who God is. In my early years of ministry, I worked in one church that had women pastors and one that had anyone of color; all the other positions were held by white males, and everyone was straight. This is a huge problem!

Whether it is a rotating group of teachers or something else, this needs to change because the second we start representing everyone from the front, the faster real transformation, understanding, and acceptance can begin. Jesus was quick to be around the people the Pharisees and Sadducees were not because he knew what they were missing. Once we actually act like everyone is made in the reflection of God, walls come down and healing begins. This does not mean going out and proselytizing to everyone, because not everyone wants Jesus, and honestly not everyone needs him, depending on who they are. Some people find refuge in him, and others don't, whether it is due to trauma or just because he's not their thing, and that is okay (contrary to what your programming may be). There are countless stories in the Bible of Jesus healing people then sending them away, being perfectly fine with them not bowing down to him. There are also stories of people that are healed because of the faith of their friends and not their own, yet Jesus is still fine with this! What does matter is how the people on Sundays or whenever, choose to participate, or how we engage with each other over the character of him?

When Jesus came on the scene, he opened up a way for those that were not born into Judaism to hitch their wagon to the redemptive work being done through that religion. It was work that should have transformed the world in a positive way. At the risk of sounding like a broken record, it prioritized caring for the poor/widow/orphan/alien, ensuring creation is taken care of, going out and finding those that are lost to themselves and helping them connect with the divine in order to fulfill their humanity, and making sure that no one went without. We have perverted that into thinking that there is a McPrayer that you say to "save" you from a fiery pit of hell that brings about torture for all time thanks to a crappy translation by someone with a political agenda (by this I specifically mean the 1611 King James Bible). We should be celebrating and partnering alongside those doing that work wherever we find them, whether or not they are doing it in his name!

I once had a debate, and I still cannot believe this, with some coworkers at a church where I worked at. They were wondering if giving food to a starving person but not sharing the Gospel (aka telling them why they need Jesus) with them was still considered a "good" thing. Are you forking kidding me? We get so in our head about this because of unhealthy theology that we ignore the person literally starving at our feet! As time goes on and we start to move past the idols of yesteryear, somethings will remain the same and that will most likely be the teachings of Jesus, whether or not our views of God reflect the times we are currently in. What we see in those teachings are the reflections of, forget God for a while and worry about the things God cares about. A lot of times, we tend to miss the forest for the trees, especially when we have been indoctrinated in a religion that does particular things for a long time. While, initially, missing the forest for the trees is not bad, however it is not the best when there are people literally starving at the door, having their kids separated at a border, or having second rate status as human beings.

I asked earlier what this looks like over time. Well, I have no idea. It will look different in all the communities that are served by it; we just need to be open. The church is terrible about dropping a frame of worship and idea of God in a culture or context where it does not fit. When things are not working, what are the sacred cows that we are not willing to lay down? Things need to change in the church, and we do not have the answer for what that will all look like, but that is okay because God is bigger than that. People aren't, but if we believe there is this thing that transcends time and space, and we are scratching at the door of it, the door will open, we just need to be brave enough to walk through.

13

Recognizing our Privilege: Prejudice, Racism, Sexism, and Ableism in the American Evangelical Church

SECTION ONE: RACISM

Over the years, this honestly has been the hardest part of my personal reconstruction. Before I restarted my career in professional ministry, when I was a pastor, I was very used to being the white savior in every situation. After all, the media I chose to consume only reflected that mentality. I personally come from a background where a lot of my family and neighbors have been blue—collar workers that moved from the coal mines of West Virginia to the auto industry or factory jobs in Northwest Ohio. When I heard about white privilege, I thought it did not reflect what I grew up with because life was still hard. But if we truly strive to live out the teachings of Jesus, then we must examine the ways we have controlled the world around us to create a utopia of comfortability. For me, part of reconstruction was realizing I was a "we can say merry Christmas again" Christian, but the Jesus in my manger was white. Placing Jesus in history helps us grow, and with growth can come pain.

I realize that as a white, CIS, heteronormative, able—bodied male that was born and lives in America, I have a certain amount of privilege that is far greater than my brothers, sisters, and non—binary who have been oppressed because of their skin color, sex, sexual orientation, and disabilities. In fact, I am probably the last person that should be writing about this subject. However, this is a vital part of reconstruction and to blow past it would be a disservice not only to those being affected by it, but also to the blinders you may have had up over the years. First of all, recognizing your privilege costs you literally nothing other than an awkward conversation with your family; rarely (if ever) does it mean excommunication from family or loved ones. These past few politically charged years have forced some of us to recognize this, and we have seen it in our institutions of worship whether intentionally or not. When Christian missionaries used to preach the "Gospel" to slaves, we would print special Bibles for them and leave things out like Moses leading the Israelites out of captivity, and the book of Revelation was not printed at all because it talked about how one day this earth will not be here, and evil will finally be punished. But our slaveholder roots would of course leave in Ephesians 6:5, conveying how servants should be good to their masters.[1]

When we start to realize our privilege and move in a way that allows us to humble ourselves it can be a bit hard, and often our feelings get hurt. There have been plenty of times when I was going through this part of reconstruction where I would specifically talk with my Black or Brown friends about race. Asking them questions thinking I was getting at the heart of the issues. In reality, I was using them to comfort my white guilt. This is unfortunately very common; we try to sit at the feet of those who look different than us in order to learn the "right" way to live, because we are so woke. Sometimes, in doing so, we make this experience about ourselves. This happens time and again. Author Austin Channing Brown talks about this in her book, *I'm Still Here: Black Dignity in a World Made for Whiteness*, saying, "This is partly what makes the fragility of whiteness so damn dangerous. It ignores the personhood of people of color and instead makes the feelings of

---

1. Little, *Bibles Given to Slaves*, line 48.

whiteness the most important thing."[2] She goes on to state that, "If Black people are dying in the street, we must consult with white feelings before naming the evils of police brutality. If white family members are being racist, we must take Grandpa's feelings into account before we proclaim our objections to such speech. If an organization's policies are discriminatory and harmful, that can only be corrected if we can ensure white people won't feel bad about the change. White fragility protects whiteness and forces Black people to fend for themselves."[3]

I know a lot of people that considered themselves good Christians that think Black Lives Matters is unneeded, unnecessary, and ignore the serious miscarriage of justice that our position of privilege allows us to ignore. When I was growing up, sometimes my family would go downtown for dinner or an event, and as soon as we got off the highway, we all had to lock our doors because we were told it was a very dangerous area. What this eventually translated to my subconscious was, if black people or other people of color are around, I am not safe, and neither is anyone or anything else, because there are criminals among them. I never considered myself racist even though I would participate in racist jokes because growing up, I was led to believe they were funny. After all, "most white people still believe that they are good and the true racists are easy to spot."[4] When you've sat in a seat of power so long and your race has predominantly been represented in media, literature, musically, and at the pulpit, equality then feels like something is being taken away.

Looking at President Obama (politics aside), he had to be one of the best in his fields in order to be elected President of the United States, and all President Trump had been a rich, white man with no qualifications. It is our responsibility to do the leg work, to read authors of color, learn from their wisdom, and call out the racist practices we see within the church and culture. Christians, ought to be leading this fight and joining our oppressed brothers, sisters,

2. Brown, *I'm Still Here*, pg. 89.
3. Brown, *I'm Still Here*, pg. 89.
4. Brown, *I'm Still Here*, pg. 101.

and non-binary because to opt into this worldview (Christianity) is to fight oppression wherever it is found head on. As James Baldwin writes in his book, *The Fire Next Time*, "In any case, white people, who had robbed black people of their liberty and who profited by this theft every hour that they lived, had no moral ground on which to stand. They had the judges, the juries, the shotguns, the law—in a word, power. But it was a criminal power to be feared but not respected, and to be outwitted in any way whatever. And those virtues preached but not practiced by the white world were merely another means of holding Negroes in subjection."[5]

It was white Christians that lynched, tortured, and tormented innocent black men, women, and children. As James H. Cone points out in his masterful book, *The Cross and the Lynching Tree*. We would have lynched Jesus if he had come back as a person of color.[6] Furthermore, we probably would have acquitted his killers if they were even to have been brought up on charges. Oppressing those we have considered the "other" has been built into our DNA, and we must overcome this. Reinhold Niebuhr, who Dr. Cone states in his book *Said I Wasn't Gonna Tell Nobody* how Niebuhr should and could have done more to call out racism,[7] and stand up against it, shows how much this is in our collective Christian blood, "If there were a drunken orgy somewhere, I would bet ten to one a church member was not in it. That is long odds, but on the whole, I would assume a church member was not in it. But if there were a lynching, I would bet ten to one a church member was in it. I don't find people belonging to churches giving a guarantee of emancipated race attitude or a high type of political morality. We can't assume that at all. We have it sometimes, but we can't assume it."[8]

I often wonder how many Christians went to church the same week they tore families apart and locked up children in the detention centers set up on the southern border.

5. Baldwin, *Fire Next Time*, pg. 23.

6. Cone, *Cross and the Lynching Tree*, pg. 31.

7. Cone, *Said I Wasn't Gonna Tell Nobody*, pg. 135.

8. Miller, *Protestant Churches and Lynching*, pg. 118.

SECTION TWO: SEXISM

Way back in the beginning of this book, I talked about how pseudepigrapha was common practice in the first century, to write in the name of an author. This is something that happened quite a bit with the letters of Paul. Unfortunately, it is because of this and the lack of critical analysis and accountability of the Bible that people often use it to oppress people, but also create second class citizenship in the kin-dom of heaven by citing passages that seemingly call to leave women out of a place of authority. Let us look at this passage in 1 Timothy 2:8–15 (NIV):

> Therefore I want the men everywhere to pray, lifting up holy hands without anger or disputing. I also want the women to dress modestly, with decency and propriety, adorning themselves, not with elaborate hairstyles or gold or pearls or expensive clothes, but with good deeds, appropriate for women who profess to worship God. A woman should learn in quietness and full submission. I do not permit a woman to teach or to assume authority over a man; she must be quiet. For Adam was formed first, then Eve. And Adam was not the one deceived; it was the woman who was deceived and became a sinner. But women will be saved through childbearing—if they continue in faith, love, and holiness with propriety.

This clobber passage has been used for hundreds and hundreds of years to keep women in a subservient position in the church. Often the churches or communities that implement this verse literally are ones that believe the entire Bible should be a literal interpretation. They are okay with implementing verse 12 literally, yet I cannot recall the last time I saw a married woman leaving her engagement or wedding band at home. After all they are usually gold, and going with the literal interpretation of this, they should therefore not adorn themselves with it. Yet, this clobber passage is perfect if you are trying to control more than half of your population. After all, it is easy to silence women when they are not allowed to speak or teach over men.

Timothy was in the modern Turkish city of Ephesus, and also located in that city was the famed Temple of Artemis, which was the main area of worship for the goddess Artemis. It was a female—centric religion, and while women were the main priests, a man could become one if he decided to castrate himself ritually and give up specific food. This was a highly religious region, and when Timothy went there to spread the word about this dead—but—not—dead guy from Jerusalem, it struck a chord with the Jewish people that were exiled there. Unfortunately, during this exile, they adopted a lot of practices that the worshipers of Artemis used as a way (they thought) to get the correct interpretations of Torah. So, this became a disruption and issue within this specific church. People were claiming to be teachers that have this understanding of Jesus and Paul used this silencing as crowd control.[9,10] It was never meant to be a policy for the church in the generations to come. After all, Paul comes from a heritage of strong and amazing women (Jael, Deborah, Esther, Tamar, and Judith just to name a few) changing the landscape of his religion and establishing the line that gave birth to the famed King David, writer of psalms and killer of Uriah.

Part of recognizing your privilege is knowing when to step down and give someone your seat at the table. Evangelicals like to talk a lot about the cost of following Jesus, but very seldom do we like to give anything up, especially the men. When we recognize that other people have been left out because of our direct treatment, we need to live up to our convictions and start really acting like we care for others.

SECTION THREE: ABLEISM

It should be pointed out, that most of this book was written in 2018, and has been updated as the years have gone on. 2020 drew a harsh line in the sand in the Christian community, not just on

9. Edwards, *Paul's Original Language*, lines 1–77.
10. Wallace, *Stop Using 1 Timothy 2:12*, lines 1–100.

the vaccine area, but the fact that there are people who cared more about not wearing a mask, then protecting those we are mandated to protect, those who are in need. What is so harrowing, is how little changed in the face of a global pandemic, and how many people leaned into the "my personal freedoms are being infringed upon" that fall in the Christian camp. What comes to mind are the worship concerts led by a long hair worship leader and Christmas carol gatherings hosted by a former child actor. Unfortunately, what follows remains largely intact from pre-pandemic times.

I touched a small bit on ableism earlier, and I am going to expand just a bit more on it. We currently live in a country where there is an argument about whether children should be vaccinated out of an unsubstantiated fear of them developing autism. Let me break that down again: there are parents who would rather their children die of a preventable disease (that parents would die *for* in other nations in order to protect their children) than for them to be what able—bodied society defines as different or "other." This is a practice I have seen embraced by the evangelical church, which honestly shouldn't be surprising since we have a difficult time embracing our siblings, especially those with disabilities. After all, unless there are non—religious meetings happening their build-ings, churches and Christian schools are not required to uphold the rules set forth from the Americans with Disabilities Act.[11] The truth is, in some cases our theology may be inclusive, but our living theology practicality has no idea what to do with disabled individuals.

Part of the reason we have no idea what to do is because Je-sus spends quite a bit of time going around and healing the sick, disabled, or possessed. This starts to create the idea that there is something inherently broken with these individuals, whether it is ever outwardly spoken or not. Social media is so happy to send out inspiration porn of disabled people doing things able—bodied people do on the regular and gives us a reason to be thankful that we are not like "them." I said this earlier but, we often only portray

11. Rose, *Churches and Handicapped Accessibility Requirements*, lines 8–16.

evangelical Christian leadership as people who are well put together, with that in mind, let us talk about Moses.

Born in a time of enslavement by the Egyptians, Moses survived the decree from Pharaoh that all male children born to the Israelites must be drowned in the Nile River. Found by Pharaoh's daughter, he is plucked from the river in his little ark (the word translated usually as basket in Exodus 2 is the same word used for Noah's Ark, the only two times this word is found in the Bible, which should bring to mind imagery of a type of salvation or rescue). After recognizing that this is a child from the Hebrews, she sends Mariam (Moses's sister, who's been watching the whole thing unfold) to find someone to nurse the child (which ends up being his mother). He is then raised in her home until he is a certain age and goes to live in Pharaoh's Palace. After he moves, some murder happens, and he flees to Midian where he meets his future wife at a well. After being invited back to her house, he starts to shepherd for his future father—in—law Jethro.

It is during a trip out into the wilderness where this story takes a turn. Moses is minding his own business when he notices a burning bush and approaches it. It is during this interaction between Moses and YHWH (who was the burning bush) that we get some very revealing information.

After Moses spends time pleading with God trying to make a case for why the Israelites won't believe him, he finally says, "Pardon your servant, Lord. I have never been eloquent, neither in the past nor since you have spoken to your servant. I am slow of speech and tongue" (Exod4:9, NIV). I had the honor of sitting in on a Sunday teaching when an acquaintance of mine, Sarah, was teaching on this passage. The teacher that morning, at the time work for a county wide board of developmental disabilities; she is also a disabled rights advocate, and she broke my mind open when she taught on this. During her teaching, she pointed out that there are some schools of thought that say Moses was disabled because of that line, and that it could go so far as a cleft palate (which is not as big of a deal if you have access to modern medicine).

She pointed out all the ways the church has been terrible about making space for those with disabilities, and we do not focus on our ableism. Even so, God still made a way and provided for Moses in his disability of speech. God makes space to go and recognize the worthiness of Moses, even when Moses does not feel worthy himself. One way it could be said is, the compromise that ends up happening is Moses acts like God in front of Pharaoh preforming acts, while Aaron (Moses's brother) is to act as Moses did providing what God was saying to let the Israelites free. The other way it could be said is, God creates accommodation and accessibility for Moses to live out his calling and grow in his gifting. God does not create a step for Moses to overcome anything, because there is nothing to overcome Moses was who he was, and God still made the space for him. God goes to greater lengths than most American evangelical church's to provide an environment for the Moses to deliver the message he was called to than evangelicalism does to provide for a disabled speaker. It is worth asking ourselves how many great theologians, preachers, etc. have we excluded from the conversation due to our inability to provide space?

SECTION FOUR: LGBTQIA+

There are a lot of clobber passages that people use in favor to try and claim why LGBTQI+ peoples are "willfully sinning." I will not be spending any time on anything Paul has written on this subject; better books have been written on that so check out the list I have provided in Appendix A and buy one from there. As one of the passages is the story of the men of Sodom, and I've already gone over that I am going to skip that whole thing, and just say feel free to reread chapter seven. Leviticus 20:13 (NRSV) reads, "If a man lies with a male as with a woman, both of them have committed an abomination; they shall be put to death—their blood is upon them." You really should not look at this passage without looking at its sister in Lev. 18:22 (NRSV), which says "You shall not lie with a male as with a woman; it is an abomination." Both passages read the same, the only difference is the capital punishment located in

20:13. Both verses are found in chapters that deal with Molech, a Canaanite god or deity. Leviticus is drawing a line between the sand on how the Canaanites worshiped their god Molech, which involved a lot of sexual aspects.[12] Along with that, this was a tribal culture that relied on reproduction to survive, so the idea of someone being born attracted to the same sex and acting upon those feelings would have been (most likely) extremely foreign and unfamiliar. Not to mention the word homosexuality didn't show up in the Christian Bible until the twentieth Century. Because of this, the passages found within Leviticus do not hold water in our current debates around this issue. Also, it is worth noting that within those chapters you find arguments for not eating shellfish, so again, similarly to the Timothy passage about women, it is all or nothing. You cannot cherry pick what is culturally relevant and what is not, no matter how much we or they may want to.

Part of realizing our privilege is looking at how we have handed down interpretations of the Bible for over a thousand years. Throughout history, we have worshiped a God we treated as dominantly male, however as discussed, God is genderless. If that is too much of a stretch, God at least identifies as both genders, because man and woman are created in the image of God. But, if people are born with both reproductive organs, does that mean they are not made in the image of God? A quick answer to that should be, "Of course they are, George, don't be silly!" What does this mean for our strict binary interpretation of the Bible? Teresa Hornsby writes (in the book she co—authored with Deryn Guest, *Transgender, Intersex, and Biblical Interpretation*), "Heteronormativity is not in the text, waiting to be discovered; the interpreter or reader brings the assumption of heteronormativity to the text and uses the text to justify heteronormativity."[13] As we rebuild our beliefs, we must always take the posture of students and ask questions not only about the text and the church, but how we have reacted to it over the years. The willingness to be open and say

12. Theology, *Religion of the Canaanites*, lines 64–66.

13. Hornsby and Guest, *Transgender, Intersex, and Biblical Interoperation*, pg. 4.

that we may be wrong, especially about gender within the Biblical narrative is key to unlocking a larger view of God and how God interacts with humanity.

As to how those identifying as Intersex (individuals born with several characteristics of sexes) fit into the church, the answer should be an easy, "everywhere." Unfortunately, not everyone is ready and willing to recognize them. We tie so much of our religion up into our physical body that it prevents us from seeing who God is, or what Jesus came to do in how to care for one another in a way that transcends physicality. Physicality is an arbitrary barrier that we allow ourselves to be stopped by in order to draw lines around who is better than who and who is in or out. Early within Christianity, people were a bit more lenient about not tying the image of God to the physical human body, "Early Christians reasoned that because God does not have a body, whatever likeness exists between humans and the divine cannot be located in the body. Therefore, they turned to concepts of the soul to tease out the meaning of the imago Dei. Following Plato and Aristotle, early Christians identified reason and virtue with the soul. God as 'all—wise' and 'all—good' was imagined in the rationality and virtue of humans."[14]

I realize that for some, the acceptance of LGBTQI+ individuals are a stretch, but we all start somewhere. When I was a kid, people thought it was "funny" to call people gay, and all of the other awful words that came with it. Being part of a larger world and worldview means there is some time for us to turn that around, make amends, and seek repentance in order to truly change. But we cannot forget that people's lives are at stake because of bad theology we held and perpetuated. To quote Justin Tanis, a transgender male, "Looking at Jesus as the one who was transformed from using epithets to healing has helped me remember that the name caller today can be the ally of tomorrow."[15] There is still hope for us yet if we allow ourselves.

14. DeFranza, *Sex Differences in Christian Theology*, pg. 118.

15. Hornsby and Guest, *Transgender, Intersex, and Biblical Interoperation*, pg. 17.

14

The Gospel . . . also Evangelism

I LOVE THE FILM *Nacho Libre* (Hess, 2006). It is about a man who is an orphan of two missionaries who tried to convert each other. As he grows into an adult, he stays on at the orphanage so he can cook for the brothers, sister, and children. At the same time, he masquerades around town as a luchador just seems right. In the movie, he complains about not being given enough priestly duties, and he says one of the best lines in the world, which really resonates with formerly young pastors I know, "they don't think I know a buttload of crap about the Gospel, but I do."[1] Which is funny because on one hand, it may be true. On the other hand, it begs the question, what actually is the Gospel? Is it the same as when I was a little kid, or does it morph as we grow older with greater understanding of a deeper world enriched with the divine?

Broadly speaking, five minutes into a church sermon about Jesus, we are almost always confronted with the word "gospel," and unfortunately most of us have no idea what means. If someone has an idea of what it means, it will most likely be a regurgitation of what was being taught, or it will vary from person to person because there is no consistent teaching. So, let's do a bit of

1. Hess, *Nacho Libre*.

a rundown of the word, and see if we can figure it out. After all, when we are rebuilding something based on the teachings of Jesus and the four books that chronicle what he did, where he went, and who he was with, are called, "The Gospel of (fill in name here)" we should have a good idea of what the heck that means. Not to get all Leslie Knope, but according to the dictionary.com, "gospel" means a several things. Here are the top four:

1. The teachings of Jesus and the apostles; the Christian revelation.

2. The story of Christ's life and teachings, especially contained in the first four books of the New Testament, namely Matthew, Mark, Luke, and John.

3. Any of these (Matthew, Mark, Luke, and John) four books.

4. Something regarded as truth and implicitly believed.

These definitions are probably familiar if you have been around any evangelical church. I have often heard "gospel" referred to the death and resurrection of Jesus, and therefore it may be intrinsically tied with evangelism. After all, it is almost impossible to bring up the gospel without mentioning or tying it somehow to evangelism or the Great Commission. Scot McKnight in his preface to *The King Jesus Gospel* had a view which I think is important point out, "Most of evangelism today is obsessed with getting someone to make a decision; the apostles, however, were obsessed with making disciples... Evangelism that focuses on decisions short circuits... aborts the design of the gospel, while evangelism that aims at disciples slows down to offer the full gospel of Jesus and the apostles."[2]

For a very long time, I thought that I had a huge problem with evangelism, in the same way I have had a great deal of struggle with Paul. However, it ends up I just haven't liked the way people have handled them! My experience with evangelism is usually the opposite: the focus is never really how far you came, but what and how you were before you made the plunge to Christianity. This

2. McKnight, *King Jesus Gospel*, 29.

often—created weird conversations, and it was always like someone was trying to "out sin" one another and brag about how great
they are now that they have changed their ways. Now, I am not saying that is the same for everyone but, with this having always been
the focus of evangelism for the sake of the gospel, I wish someone
would have told me I would want to watch porn equally as much
before and after conversion when things are really, really rough.
But we have cheapened both the gospel and evangelism through
this catchall called Jesus.

As a young pastor I had to report my conversion numbers for
my weekly ministry report, for our total church report that went
up to the denomination's conference headquarters. At the time, the
head of conference was obsessed with evangelism and conversion,
which I suppose is a good thing if you think people are going to
hell and a prayer can save them. If our numbers of conversions
dipped, we were probably doing something wrong. One month in
particular, I remember this being a huge issue because the conference head was on the path to save everyone. He came to our
church and gave an old school fire and brimstone sermon, and I
felt incredibly uncomfortable. The idea of showing up in people's
lives, giving this mammoth of a teaching, then abandoning them
and leaving it for others to walk them down this path just felt so
sleazy.

I will never forget the one time I "led" to a person to Christ
in my adult life as a religious professional, it felt so weird. Here
was this adult guy, and I was told that if I met anyone wanting to
"dedicate their life to Christ" I needed to walk them through it and
some type of prayer. It was this moment when I was like, "okay,
what the heck is the gospel? This feels wrong since people are still
starving in the world. It cannot only be an afterlife only thing."

The word evangelist is found three times in the Bible, all of
which are located in the New Testament. First, in Acts 21:8 referring to Philip the Evangelist, then Ephesians 4:11 referring to the
people Jesus gave authority to, and finally, 2 Timothy 4:5, referring
to the work that needs done. This word in Greek is εὐαγγελιστής
and means a bringer of good news. This definition was not specific

to religion, but Christians used this word more than any other group, it's become universally associated with our worldview. All it originally meant was that there was a piece of information meant to be received as good in a way that would impact lives positively. The question that we should ask ourselves when faced with this information is, what is this good news that evangelism is supposed to bring versus what I have known it to be.

Because so often it is tied to the Great Commission, here is a reminder where the great commission is pulled from, Matthew 28:16–20 (NIV), "Then the eleven disciples went to Galilee, to the mountain where Jesus had told them to go. When they saw him, they worshiped him; but some doubted. Then Jesus came to them and said, 'All authority in heaven ad on earth has been given to me. Therefore go and make disciples of all nations, baptizing them in the name of the Father and of the Son and of the Holy Spirit, and teaching them to obey everything I have commanded you. And surely I am with you always, to the end of the age.'"

Very often, Christians treat the great commission as this quick thing to try and "save" more people by going around and evangelizing, spreading the good news about the gospel. The issue with this is, when people pop in, drop what can be severely life—changing information, and leave, it can mess a person up. We ignore the most basic and time-consuming part of the command: discipleship. We often mix up discipleship with mentorship. Discipleship takes a long time to develop, and if done right, it takes on its own way of life. The idea is that you are bestowing your knowledge and applying your believe and behave to be one action. So, when we instead decide to turn the great commission into evangelism it becomes cheap and unrecognizable thing. When we focus on real discipleship instead, it becomes this long and arduous journey unlike what we have seen it become today in the church. After all, since this is supposed to be the work of the spreading of the gospel, what is the message that is worth spending so much time working on? One more quote from Scot McKnight's book, *The King Jesus Gospel*, "Evangelicalism is known for at least two words: gospel and (personal) salvation . . . we evangelicals (mistakenly) equate the word gospel with the word salvation . . . evangelicals see the word gospel, our instinct is to think (personal) 'salvation.' We are wired this way. But these two words don't mean the same thing."[3]

The gospel is the good news that we are supposed to be delivering in accordance with the great commission. St Francis is attributed to saying, "preach the gospel at all times, when necessary, use words." So, what action could speak so loudly that we may never have to talk about why we are doing what we are doing? One way of answering is bringing justice to those that do not have it. Think about it—what does Jesus spend his time doing? Teaching others a new way of life, one that elevates others and honors them while ensuring that those who are marginalized are taken care of. He announces this new way of life that flips the power structures on its head so now the last will be first, and we are invited into participating in this new kin-dom on earth. One that rejects power and social gain in favor of helping those who are in need whatever that means for the context you are in. This entrance into our full humanity by joining arm and arm with those doing this work is an example of what this new life could look like in the age to come. This work takes a long time to do and learn. There is a reason why we use the term salvation; there is a physicality that people are getting saved from, not just some spiritual idea of a far—off land after we die (which we will talk about in the next chapter).

For a long time, whenever I heard the word or even said evangelism, my entire body would go tight, and people could tell I was physically uncomfortable. All I could think about is the televangelist and how terribly they set back Christianity in America. When I started to learn about the physicality of evangelism because of learning the gospel was more than a spiritual thing, my perspective changed greatly. If we decide to participate in this great commission of going out and making disciples of all nations, we must do so physically. Clothe the naked, feed the hungry, bring dignity and justice to those without it. This may mean showing up to protest unjust decisions or anything that denies someone their humanity. After all, if we believe all people are made in the image

3. McKnight, *King Jesus Gospel*, pg. 29.

of God then we must act like it and share that and use words when necessary. This version of the gospel is much more complicated than when it was just telling people they are sinners who need saving from hellfire and brimstone. We must show up in a way we were never taught or prepared for. So yes, the gospel is the good news that we are invited into this story and practice of Jesus. The good news that things do not have to be the way they are currently. Good news that corruption will only last so long. Good news that when we interact with the gospel we and others are changed for the better physically, which transforms, transcends, and includes our emotional and spiritual wellbeing in a way that it previously did not.

15

The Fire Down Below
and the Kin-dom at Hand

To SPEAK BROADLY AND a bit hyperbolically, I think most of us have been to a gathering or funeral where, at some point, the person in charge started a sentence with, "If you were to die here, today, right now, do you know where your eternal soul would go? Would you, because you're a hopeless sinner, born in original sin and depravity, spend eternity in the pits of Hell, tortured with the likes of Hitler, Gandhi, all the tribes and people that have either never heard, or rejected the Gospel and saving power of Jesus, or would you go to Heaven? Will you spend your eternal days in glory and light where there are many mansions, and the streets are paved with gold? Have you said the prayer to let Jesus, son of God, enter your heart to become your close, personal savior? Are you ready to let your salvation story, to become more powerful, thanks to the fire pits of Hell where God sends his enemies?" I'm sorry, I can't do this anymore. This is what I grew up around when I was brought to church and almost every funeral since then (that I haven't officiated). Most of the time when evangelicals talk about Jesus in these scenarios, they want to talk about how the world is fallen and Jesus provides fire insurance from the flames of hell, which he spends very little time talking about. But where do these images come from? Who decided what the afterlife was like and who gets to be there? Where did the imagery from the famous Renaissance era paintings come from?

When we are reconstructing our faith, one thing in the back of our minds, at least for myself, is what do we actually do with the previously learned knowledge of what happens when we die? Because let's face it, when most people we know die, we would like to think they have gone on to see their loved ones who preceded them in death. We want to know we will see our children, or parents, friends, grandparents, etc. when we die. For almost two thousand years, this idea helped to sell people on Christianity as well as being a tool to keep people in submission. In this chapter we are going to go over some of that. At the end of the day, I will not tell you what to believe, I will share where I am at with this, but your journey is yours alone. All we know is that there is this nearly impenetrable veil between this world and what lies beyond that religion has been trying to help us address since the beginning of time.

In ancient Judaism, there are a few accounts of what happens after one dies. Whether or not a person is righteous or unrighteous, they refer to Sheol, a place of silence as their destination. Sheol is translated quite often into the English has "hell," especially in the Hebrew Bible. Within the Old Testament, Sheol is described in five different ways. The first is as an "unseen realm of the dead."[1] We see this example in Genesis 37:35 when Jacob is mourning for Joseph, and Sheol is described as a place he will go to in mourning for his son. The second is a literal "grave"[2] described in Numbers 16:30 (NRSV), "But if the LORD creates something new, and the ground opens its mouth and swallows them up, with all that belongs to them, and they go down alive into Sheol then you shall know that these men despised the LORD" The third way Sheol is referenced is as a specific place to punish the wicked, a place of spiritual death, or complete separation from God. Psalm 55:15 is an example of this: "let them go down alive to the realm of the dead, for evil finds

1. Stewart, *What is Sheol?*, line 13.
2. Stewart, *What is Sheol?*, line 14.

lodging among them" (NIV). The prophet Habakkuk 2:5 compares it to an appetite that cannot be contained, "because he is as greedy as the grave and like death is never satisfied" (NIV). In this way, it is more of a symbolic place. Finally, the fifth description is of a place those who are righteous are rescued from. "For great is your steadfast love toward me; you have delivered me from the depths, from the realm of the dead" (Psalm 86:13, NIV).

Another school of thought on Sheol is that it is a more symbolic place within the bowels of the earth where it is an oblivion—like place instead of where spirits retain a sense of self and live. However, in Daniel 12:2 there is the idea that the dead are just asleep until they are to awake to either life everlasting or something a little darker. Because of this, there were some who thought that during a messianic age either everyone will be resurrected and judged accordingly (sound familiar?), leaving the righteous to carry on, or a partial resurrection. During the period of Second Temple Judaism, because of a passage found in the book of Daniel, the idea of an immortal soul began to enter into thought, which was explored upon by rabbis.[3] Because this is where our understanding of hell within Christianity was born out of, we should take a look at these ideas. There is a generally accepted idea that after Jesus died, he descended to the realm of the dead for three days and set free, or rescued, those souls who were trapped in Sheol. After that, he appeared as a gardener outside of the tomb. Now, it is well known that in his teachings, Jesus also compared things to hell, or Gehenna (not just cities in Ohio and Michigan). What is this place that Jesus described as the opposite of the kin-dom he was trying to bring forth, the same kin-dom that John the Baptist was claiming that was at hand in his day?

Located in Jerusalem was a valley called Gehenna. This valley was a location where previous kings would sacrifice their children, which was expressly forbidden within Torah to do. In fact, in Isaiah 30:33 and 66:24, Gehenna was mentioned as the fiery pit in which God's enemy's bodies will burn in an un—quenching fire. It was also a garbage pit where the flames never went out, they

3. My Jewish Learning, *Life After Death*, lines 45–54.

just simmered under the surface. Described in vivid detail, Dr. Sharon Putt (Baker) has this to say in her book, *Razing Hell*, "New garbage was piled on top of the old decaying garbage: rotting fish, slimy vegetation, decaying human refuse of every imaginable sort. And as you know from experience, a dump without flies is a dump without garbage. The flies laid eggs on the surface of the dump. So just imagine the hundreds of thousands of squirmy, wormy maggots living there, eating the rotting refuse. All the while, under the surface, the fire still burned, devouring the putrid garbage days and weeks past."[4]

So, we can safely assume anytime Jesus is talking about the kin-dom of heaven, it is meant to be the opposite of this idea. This imagery is very striking, but moreover, it was a very physical place. Now, I must point out that a quick web browser search will show you that as of yet, there is no physical evidence for this fiery pit outside of Jerusalem. In fact, this is part of what Francis Chan jumped on *Love Wins* about (which was kind of interesting at the time that this happened because in my circles, that particular camp was not known for being concerned for historical accuracy, and context in which the Bible was written).

Even in spite of this information, it is still thought by many that the existence of Gehenna, also known as the Valley of Hinnom, is still plausible and an important part of the tradition to keep using.[5] The imagery of Gehenna in Mark 9:43–48 is consistent with the idea of it in Isaiah, so while no physical evidence remains of this pit, the imagery is undeniable (and do not forget that the power of imagery was and still is prominent within the Hebrew text). Jesus pointed out that not participating in the kin-dom here and now was like living a life in Gehenna, not Sheol, which was the traditional idea of the afterlife. Given this background behind this imagery of "hell," how did it graduate to where it is at now? After all, in each of these cases, there is no mention of the devil, or anyone ruling over it.

4. Putt, *Razing Hell*, pg. 129.

5. Perriman, *Was Gehenna a Burning Rubbish Dump and Does it Matter?*, lines 38–41.

On Munday Thursday in the year 1300, just before the dawn of Good Friday, poet Dante Alighieri wrote that he was lost in the woods. Now this may be hard to believe, but during this time, while the Roman Catholic Church was in charge and running day—to—day life, they may have not been as great as they wanted their followers to believe they were. I know what you're thinking, but believe it or not, absolute power has the ability to corrupt—well intentioned people absolutely. And while Dante wasn't always the best person (for example, maneuvering his influence to help banish or exile some of his competitors), he and his family were banished from his home of Florence. Dante actually appealed to the Pope to reverse this and was denied, and in return while trying to make his way in exile, he wrote the *Divine Comedy*.

What transpires in part one of his epic *Divine Comedy* is his journey through the nine circles of hell (eventually ending up in paradise). Dante finds himself navigating with Virgil through limbo, lust, gluttony, greed, wrath, heresy, violence, fraud, and treachery. It is because of this experience that you can see so many popular figures from his time, including six Popes he condemned to hell, throughout the narrative. It was a hugely popular piece of art that still influences art and culture to this day.[6,7] In fact, another popular piece of art that inspired a lot of our modern view of hell, similarly to the *Divine Comedy* was written by a man named John Milton, and that little piece of work is called *Paradise Lost*.

These epic poems that were, in effect, commentaries on the times, led to an influence that would cause imaginations to run wild about the horrors that awaited after death. Embellishing these stories and the theology of the day was very useful in controlling crowds and classes of people. I will never forget when I was sitting in a meeting with other pastors in the conference I worked for, when one of them lamented that we should bring back the fire and brimstone to scare more people back into the pews (during a conversation about declining church attendance and the stress of finances). Dying is scary, but not knowing if anything happens

6. History, *Dante Exiled from Florence*, lines 1–23.
7. Graves, *Dante Banished*, lines 1–36.

after death can be scarier. But it is nothing short of cruel to holding people in fear of a place we've completely misinterpreted due to pop culture, especially considering how hard daily life is. Let's talk about the kin-dom that is at hand

Whether or not we decide to be a part of it, the kin-dom of heaven is currently at hand. It is happening right now while we tend to our organic urban gardens, and dump plastic by the tons killing innocent sea life. In my years around the church, this subject is usually glazed over as a faraway idea, and it usually leads into a conversation about salvation. The thing that I have never understood is how a traditional salvation conversation can happen within the context of Jesus' message that the kin-dom of heaven is at hand. Once the evangelical surface is scratched off (the repent your sins and be saved by Jesus) there seems to be more there than people want to admit, because while we do not know what exactly the kin-dom of heaven looks like on earth, we can guess, and our best guess is that it is hard work. Where do we start? Let's look at what we already know.

Community has been a tenant of the practice in Christianity since its inception. We should know that we are supposed to gather together regularly and engage with those we gather with. These interactions ought to change our outlook on life. Things we thought we knew about walks of life should be challenged by those who have actually been there. Jesus' idea of the kin-dom of heaven implies we are growing closer to one another and living in community with God in mind. Doing the work that God cares about, the things that we were made to do (are you sick of me talking about this yet?): caring for those who either cannot care for themselves, are seeking a better life and ways to go about it, the poor, the hungry, the orphan, the widow, and the foreigner. This does not mean that we have to sell everything and join a commune together, but it does mean is we should evaluate how we live our highly individualized lives in a holistic and meaningful way (not just for the social media likes).

This is why discipleship is such an important part to the kin-dom of heaven; it changes how we align our beliefs and our behavior, and it impacts what we do with our dollars and cents. Those of us who have the privilege to, we should evaluate where we buy our food, our clothes, how we get around the city we live in. As we rebuild our faith and put it into action, we should think about our theologies on the environment, consumerism, relationships, and other far—reaching areas of our life. What we do and say, says a lot about what we believe and follow. Especially in a society in which we are all supposed to be "free" to make decisions for ourselves, seeing our neighbors who still are second class citizens (typically anyone that is not a straight, cis, white male) suffering from injustice is a kin-dom matter we ought to attend to. Also, worth noting when we die, we don't go to a place that is permanent. If we believe that there will be a new heaven and earth remade at the end of all things then it stands to reason that if we go anywhere at all immediately after death, it is no more than a waiting room. So, it matters what we do with the here and now, how we respond to injustice, how we forgive each other, how we tend to the land we were given to watch over. It all matters.

16

Growth, Change, and Discipleship

As stated throughout this book, this project has taken several years to get to the hands of the readers. With every edit that I went through, or my first editor Lindsey, a chapter or section would be dropped or rearranged. Not because the content was something I did not want to share, but it just did not seem to fit. For example, there is an entire chapter on Judas Iscariot I couldn't keep, much to my disappointment because it had grown into a project all its own. But all of that is okay because it is the way growth and change works. There are seasons of our lives where go through this as well. As my councilor once put it during a similar season I had experienced, it was like trying to wear a jacket that did not quite fit, and I would not stop trying to make it fit. But that is an area the church, and our leaders have failed us collectively. And that is when it's time to say goodbye.

I have always found it incredibly hypocritical for the evangelical church to talk about an individual's faith journey, like it is an actual ongoing journey with no finished destination, but when one has outgrown the framework, they are the one that is shamed and wrong. For people who are wanting to walk further down the path of this journey, it can be a hard transition., especially when the church has become a corporation. That is something that is incredibly difficult when being a Christian in the United States, the co—opting of God in the name of capitalism. There have been so many movements within the church in the past 100 years that have come and gone. Unfortunately, some of them had made a lot of money and there is the need to perpetuate this movement, hopefully it is not done out of greed (even though we know it has and can happen). But the belief is that people need to experience God this way because of the good that was done in the lives of the people who lived through it.

There are so many churches in the area I live and work that should have closed their doors and combined congregations a long time ago, but it will probably never happen. They keep meeting and doing the same things they have done for decades living out their own little corner of whatever kin-dom of heaven they have created for themselves. This is not to say those churches are not doing good works and that God is still present in those spaces, but the practicality of aging and building maintenance is a real issue. But at the heart of this issue of growth and leaving a place is the same issue that has been at the heart of Christianity since its inception. It is the question of, is the work of the church making disciples or winning converts?

Converts stay in the area drinking the Jesus juice. They come to get fed, and they leave when the teaching or meal is over with. We see the crowds following Jesus throughout the gospels, and he does not seem to have a problem with them, they are as welcomed as anyone else, but there is incredibly little expected of them. That is not the case with disciples. There is an expectation to go deeper and further than others. When we remove the context of Jesus' time, we forget we cannot draw a one—to—one comparison to ourselves (newly converted or other) and the disciples or followers of Jesus. In their book, *Sitting at the Feet of Rabbi Jesus: How the Jewishness of Jesus can Transform your Faith*, Lois Tverberg and Ann Spangler get into the specifics of what life would have looked like for those that Jesus called to a longer journey.

First, they would have studied Torah and had it memorized by the age of 5 or 6, which was common for most boys. After that, around age 10, they would have gone on to study the Oral Law, which were rules that were set up as a buffer around Torah. The idea and intent being there was such a reverence and respect for the Torah and the blessings of instructions on how to live, to avoid missing the mark there was a buffer set up so they wouldn't fall into sinning.[1] From there, around age 13, for most of the boys, they would learn their families trade, and continue with their lives, start a family, have kids, etc. However, those who were very talented would go on to study at their local synagogue, and the best of those would go on to become a disciple of a teacher or rabbi.[2] It was also believed that the mark of a good student, which would translate to a good teacher, was the ability to argue well.

This is something I brought up previously, but it is worth noting again. Jesus arguing with the Pharisees was a common practice. Debating with one another about the meaning of the text was a way to discover truth. This practice is something that has been called arguing for the sake of heaven.[3] Finally, the goal of a teacher at this time would be to become, "a living example of what it means to apply God's Word to one's life"[4] and to pass that on to their students.[5] To summarize, someone who was well versed in the Torah, the oral tradition, could argue well, and live in a way that meant applying God's words to their life. With all that in mind, we find Jesus telling people to follow and learn from him.

This is groundwork that was laid for his disciples before Jesus said let's go fishing for people. When we think about how ill prepared the church made us for figuring out when it is time to call things quits, all this factors into it. The disciples were sent out by Jesus with only the clothes on their backs to see if they had really absorbed what he had taught them. If the towns did not like what they were selling, they were instructed to call it quits and shake the dust of that town off and head out. Most of us were not taught

1. Spangler and Tverberg, *Sitting at the Feet of Rabbi Jesus*, pg. 24.

2. Spangler and Tverberg, *Sitting at the Feet of Rabbi Jesus*, pg. 25.

3. Sacks, *Argument for the sake of Heaven*, lines 1–10.

4. Spangler and Tverberg, *Sitting at the Feet of Rabbi Jesus*, pg. 33.

5. Spangler and Tverberg, *Sitting at the Feet of Rabbi Jesus*, pg. 33.

that. Most of us have been taught that what leadership says goes, and you are not to question or argue with it even though those concepts are baked into our very beginnings. There is an argument to be made that we have almost 2,000 years' worth of history to draw upon when trying to figure out how to reform our churches and theologies, but as most of us have experienced, sometimes you just need a wrecking ball so it can begin again from scratch.

There is no blueprint for where we are at in post—deconstruction, reconstruction, re—deconstruction, or re—reconstruction. All I know is, I believe Christianity has the best language for me when it comes to the deepest mysteries of the universe. I truly believe that the teachings of Jesus could make all our lives better, because a life lived pursuing justice and safety for those without it, is a life worth living. This means that we will need to leave our homes as we are called out into the world to live these practices out. The church is changing so much in our generation that it is incredibly hard to figure out where the solid ground is. Discerning this, is why discipleship over conversion is so important. It prepares you for the deeper and longer journeys this faith life has in store, and growth is naturally a part of that. It is easy for me to sit and write about outgrowing a spiritual home or finding a different community, but I have walked that path. It is incredibly difficult, but so is being honest with ourselves and not letting resentment grow because others are not asking the same questions that we are.

Change is never easy, and growth can be tiring, but I believe in your ability. Do not be afraid to go out and find the jacket that fits you, not only will it feel better, but you will look great in it.

17

This Is Where I Leave You

OUR FAITH IS AN ever growing and ever-changing thing, and that is okay. It is beautiful, but it is also important to know where you came from and that some of those aspects of it may be good and worth keeping. This is why deconstruction and reconstruction are so hard. Once this door is open, it is a lifelong ordeal. As I have said, there is no place to "arrive" to, just ever constant states of deconstructing what you have put together and reconstructing aspects of that rubble again. It may not be as destructive as before, but like a home, there are always things you want to touch up, or update. Every time I get a few steps down the road thinking I have it all together, I find there is a rock in my theological shoe, and I have to stop to rework that area again. There is a lot we have to reconcile with our faith as we move forward that this book has barely scratched the surface of.

Early on in our faith journeys, we are taught to be so concerned about what is right and what is wrong that we lose the idea that it is okay to be uncertain. After all, for some of us, we are taught being uncertainty is a bad thing. There are gray areas within Christianity, and they will continue to be there long after we have shaken this mortal coil. So, with all of this in mind, how do we move forward? How can a life lived previously in the security of

God's love bring us to a new fulfilling way of being? I have no clue, but I can tell you what has worked for me.

While writing the first draft of this book, my wife asked me a question while we were out to eat one evening. "How would your life be different if you actually believed Jesus was coming back in your lifetime?" This caught me completely off guard. This isn't one of those questions you wrestle with post—deconstruction, because it seems like it is so arbitrary. After all, I have read so many books, studied the Greek and Hebrew passages of the Bible, I think I know a lot! So why would I consider Jesus ever to come back in this life? He hasn't shown up in almost two thousand years after all. So why did this question take me back so much?

When people ask my thoughts on the second coming, I usually like to say that I live in the hope of a reconciliation of all things before I die. So, when the one person I couldn't fool with that answer asked me about my real thoughts, I was speechless. After all, I claim to want to imitate Jesus' teachings and actions in this life, so why was it such a hard question about how I act and live now? In my former search for knowledge and my current search for understanding, I have ignored something very important, which is how I treat others in spite (or because) of what I learn. My reconstruction left out the betterment of my fellow humans. And I'm not just talking about the ones who are on the receiving end of injustice but also those who are the oppressors.

There is a prayer in the Gospel of Matthew (6:9–15) that we often recite but ignore the implications and actions required of it, not to mention the lines that follow it, "Our Father in heaven, hallowed be your name. Your kingdom come. Your will be done, on earth as it is in heaven. Give us this day our daily bread. And forgive us our debts, as we also have forgiven our debtors. And do not bring us to the time of trial, but rescue us from the evil one" (Matt 6:9–13, NRSV).

For me, this is a terrifying passage. Forgive our debts, as we also have forgiven our debtors? Are you serious? In the same way that I forgive someone, I am to be forgiven in that measure. And then it goes on and finishes with, "for if you forgive others their trespasses, your heavenly Father will also forgive you; but if you do not forgive others, neither will your Father forgive you" (Matt 6:14–15, NRSV). So, this forgiveness thing and the way I go about it is apparently very crucial for my faith journey. This area of the Sermon on the Mount is often in the "we will get to it eventually" pile of sermons because (broadly speaking) the American evangelical church doesn't know how to, not only address healthy boundaries, or grasp forgiveness. The American evangelical church thrives off of unhealthy boundaries! It's how we are able to pay pastors and ministry directors below the poverty line and we burn out volunteers so easily. It is also the same reason we ignore the "love your enemies and pray for those who persecute you" passage. This is why the question of how I would live if I actually believed Jesus was going to come back in my lifetime was so hard to answer. I would have to confront not only the parts of text I ignore, but the way my life is actually lived out! So not only am I stuck reconstructing what and how I believe, I am also still reconstructing how I act.

The thing I was struck with most was how much fear was still in me about Jesus coming back before my death. Am I living a life that I'd be proud to say is Jesus—inspired? Well, obviously not all the time. I mean, I did have someone tattoo an Ewok on my forearm, so there is that. But as a whole, does my theology match up with my every day? Of course, it doesn't. Sitting with the question though, I am reminded of something that has been coming to mind over and within the past sixteen months. There is, what I believe a very important but also kind of throw away passage that I did not realize was impacting the question my wife asked me. Simon (Peter) talks to Jesus after the resurrection, and it essentially goes like this:

> Jesus: Simon, do you love me?
> Simon: Yes Lord.
> Jesus: Feed my lambs.
> —beat—
> Jesus: Simon, do you love me?
> Simon: Uh, yes Lord, of course I love you.

Jesus: Take care of my sheep.
—beat—
Jesus: Simon, do you love me?
Simon: Of course, I love you Lord!
Jesus: Then feed my sheep.

For me, this interaction I have paraphrased from John 21 should be part of the foundation of every reconstruction. It is incredibly important to figure out who we are and what we believe post—deconstruction. However, if we are not being propelled forward in helping our fellow humans, then what is the point of staying within the Christian camp?

We don't have the luxury of seeing Jesus' face to face post—resurrection like his disciples. Our reconstruction and next steps in this journey are done with fear and trembling, not because of, "what if we are wrong?" but more out of, "what if we are right?" That is a terrifying thought in a country where there is an uncomfortable number of Christians will say you are no longer a part of their family because you do not agree with their tenants of faith. This is *mostly* uncharted territory, and we are getting back to looking at God in ways people haven't since the pre—Enlightenment and Victorian eras. What if we are right that we will never know who God fully is? This is where the evangelical in me says, "That's okay because we have Jesus." That doesn't mean we ignore the fullness of God, who God isn't, and switching up God's pronoun to properly engage with our divine Mother.

Our reconstruction should be about taking doors off hinges, opening windows of the houses we have built on our new foundation, and constantly building a longer table so that we may invite others to this meal and never run out of room. I realize how pie in the sky this sounds but in order to change what we have known; we must be willing to act as if Jesus is coming back in this lifetime. Not in the John the Baptist, repent because the kin-dom of heaven is here type of brow beating. But as if Jesus shows up and recognizes the kin-dom being at hand because of our work. Ultimately, we have no idea how this will look, but we do know that kindness, justice, community, and inclusion will be a part of it. Faith is a personal thing. For me, I am living in this uncertainty and just trying to not be a loud person veiled in Christianity justifying why I can treat the poor like crap and not fight for equality of my LGBTQIA+, racially different, differently abled fellow citizens in this kin-dom.

Reconstructed Christianity means recognizing that my freedom and salvation are wrapped up in others, and I need to work with them to free them from the bonds I helped uphold.

Reconstruction means having uncomfortable conversations and cutting out toxic people during Thanksgiving with my family and maintaining healthy boundaries.

Reconstruction is reading Mark and being okay with the resurrection being left out because I am fighting for a better tomorrow in the way of my teacher, never knowing he is coming back.

Reconstruction is my debt being forgiven in the same way I have forgiven my debtors.

Reconstruction is finding and feeding the sheep.

May you know that this work will never be done, but always worth doing, may you see yourself in the long story of God participating in creation, and may you know the grace and peace of a kin-dom lifestyle through all the turmoil we are handed on a daily basis.

Grace and peace be with you.

Appendix A

While there may be others named in this book, out of every book I have listed, these are what I would consider required reading:

The Fire Next Time by James Baldwin

The Cross and the Lynching Tree by James Cohn

Dear Church by Lenny Duncan

Transforming by Austen Hartke

Sex Difference in Christian Theology by Megan DeFranza

The Great Emergence by Phyllis Tickle

The Early History of God by Mark S. Smith

Transgender, Intersex, and Biblical Interpretation by Teresa J. Hornsby and Deryn Guest

Everyman's Talmud by Abraham Cohen

Stamped from the Beginning by Ibram X. Kendi

God in Search of Man by Abraham Heschel

The Sabbath by Abraham Heschel

The Talmud

The Five Books of Miriam by Ellen Frankel

Sitting at the Feet of Rabbi Jesus by Lois Tverberg

Appendix A

Inspired by Rachel Held Evans

What Is the Bible by Rob Bell

Bibliography

Brannan, R. "Writing a Systematic Theology? You Must Discuss These References." https://academic.logos.com/writing-a-systematic-theology-you-must-discuss-these-references/

Biale, D. "The God with Breasts: El Shaddai in the Bible." *History of Religions*, vol. 21, no. 3, University of Chicago Press, 1982, pp. 240-56, http://www.jstor.org/stable/1062160.

Brown, A.C. *I'm Still Here Black Dignity in a World Made for Whiteness.* New York City: Crown, 2018.

Baldwin, J. *The Fire Next Time.* New York City: Penguin Random House, 1963.

Burns, J.E. "Pharisees and Rabbinic Judaism" https://www.bibleodyssey.org/en/people/related-articles/pharisees-and-rabbinic-judaism

Concannon, C. "Paul and Authorship" https://www.bibleodyssey.org:443/people/related-articles/paul-and-authorship.

Cone, J.H. *Said I wasn't Gonna Tell Nobody the Making of a Black Theologian.* Ossining: Orbis, 2018

Cone, J.H. *The Cross and the Lynching Tree.* Ossining: Orbis, 2013.

DeFranza, M. *Sex Difference in Christian Theology: Male, Female, and Intersex in the Image of God.* Grand Rapids: Eerdmans, 2015.

Dictionary. "Gospel." https://www.dictionary.com/browse/abba#:~:text=an%20Aramaic%20word%20for%20father,a%20relation%20of%20personal%20intimacy.

Edwards, B. "1 Timothy 2: Paul's Original Language, Timothy's Original Context" https://juniaproject.com/1-timothy-pauls-language-original-context/

Evangebros. "Breisheet." https://evangebros.podbean.com/e/breisheet-portions-week-one/

Evangebros. "Noach." https://music.amazon.com/podcasts/4d0bb7b8-be98-480a-9104-044c9552b71d/episodes/7dd19389-a493-4932-bc0b-c3cf052151e4/evangebros-noach-torah-portions-week-two?

Greenwald, A. "Your Brother's Blood Cries Out at Me From the Ground!" https://www.aju.edu/ziegler-school-rabbinic-studies/our-torah/back-issues/your-brothers-blood-cries-out-me-ground.

Guthrie, W. "Jesus Christ." https://www.woodyguthrie.org/Lyrics/Jesus_Christ. htm.

Graves, D. "Dante Banished Wrote the Divine Comedy." https://www. christianity.com/church/church-history/timeline/1201-1500/dante-banished-wrote-the-divine-comedy-11629851.html

Hinson, T. *Documentary Hypothesis: An Examination of JEDP Theory*. Self Published.

Hebrew4Christians. "The Names of God." https://www.hebrew4christians.com/ Names_of_G-d/El/el.html.

History. "Dante is Exiled from Florence" https://www.history.com/this-day-in-history/dante-is-exiled-from-florence

Hornsby, T. and Deryn Guest. *Transgender, Intersex, and Biblical Interpretation*. Atlanta: SBL, 2016

Jewish Encyclopedia. "Names of God." http://www.jewishencyclopedia.com/ articles/11305-names-of-god.

Just, F. "The Duetero-Pauline Letters" https://www.catholic-resources.org/ Bible/Paul-Disputed.htm

Lexicon-Concordance. http://lexiconcordance.com/hebrew/6595.html

Little, B. "Why Bibles Given to Slaves Omitted Most of the Old Testament" https://www.history.com/news/slave-bible-redacted-old-testament.

Maimonides, Touger, E. (Editor). *Pirkei Avot*. Brooklyn, NY: Moznaim, 1994

Mark, J. "Enuma Elish the Babylonian Epic of Creation." https://www.ancient. eu/article/225/enuma-elish---the-babylonian-epic-of-creation---fu/.

———https://www.ancient.eu/article/221/the-mesopotamian-pantheon/.

McKnight, S. *The King Jesus Gospel the Original Good News Revisited*. Grand Rapids: Zondervan, 2016.

My Jewish Learning, "Life After Death" https://www.myjewishlearning.com/ article/life-after-death/.

My Jewish Learning. "The Tetragrammaton." https://www.myjewishlearning. com/article/the-tetragrammaton/.

Miller, R.M. "The Protestant Churches and Lynching, 1919-1939." *The Journal of Negro History* 42, no. 2 (1957): 118-31. https://doi.org/10.2307/2715687.

Nacho Libre, directed by Jared Hess (2006; Hollywood, CA: Paramount Pictures Distrobution, 2006), DVD.

Nietzsche, F. "The Mad Man." https://sourcebooks.fordham.edu/mod/nietzsche -madman.asp.

Perriman, A. "Was Gehenna a Burning Rubbish Dump, and Does it Matter?" https://www.postost.net/2015/11/was-gehenna-burning-rubbish-dump-does-it-matter.

Pines, S. "An Arabic Version of Testimonium Flavianum and Its Implications" http://khazarzar.skeptik.net/books/pines01.pdf.

Poblete, C. "The Names of God: Qanna" https://blogs.blueletterbible.org/blb/ 2012/08/28/the-names-of-god-qanna/.

Putt, S. *Razing Hell: Rethinking Everything You've Been Taught About God's Wrath and Judgement*. Louisville: Westminster John Knox, 2010

Rose, V. "Churches and Accessibility Requirements." https://www.cga.ct.gov/2006/rpt/2006-R-0756.htm.

Spangler, A., and Lois Tverberg. *Sitting at the Feet of Rabbi Jesus How the Jewishness of Jesus can Transform your Faith.* Grand Rapids: Zondervan, 2009.

Sacks, J. "Argument for the Sake of Heaven" https://rabbisacks.org/argument-for-the-sake-of-heaven-korach-5779/.

Steinsaltz, Adin. *Talmudic Images.* Jerusalem: Koren, 2010.

Stewart, D. "What is Sheol?" https://www.blueletterbible.org/faq/don_stewart/don_stewart_1_3.cfm.

Theology. "The Religion of the Canaanites." https://www.theology.edu/canaan.htm.

Wallace, G. "5 Reasons to Stop using 1 Timothy 2:12 Against Women." https://juniaproject.com/5-reasons-stop-using-1-timothy-212-against-women/.

Weinfeld, M. "The Covenant of Grant in the Old Testament and in the Ancient near East." *Journal of the American Oriental Society* 90, no. 2 (1970): 184-203. https://doi.org/10.2307/598135.